THE USBORNE BOOK OF
FAMOUS
ARTISTS

THE USBORNE BOOK OF
FAMOUS ARTISTS

Ruth Brocklehurst,
Rosie Dickins and Abigail Wheatley

Designed by Nicola Butler
Drawings by Mark Beech
Art consultant: Kathleen Adler

This photograph shows a close-up of Monet's paint palette.

Contents

About this book   5
Giotto   6
Jan van Eyck   8
Leonardo da Vinci   10
Albrecht Dürer   14
Michelangelo   16
Raphael   19
Titian   22
Hans Holbein   24
Bruegel   26
El Greco   28
Caravaggio   30
Peter Paul Rubens   32
Rembrandt   35
Diego Velázquez   38
Jan Vermeer   40
Goya   42
J.M.W. Turner   44
Eugène Delacroix   46
John Everett Millais   48

Edouard Manet   50
Edgar Degas   52
Claude Monet   54
Pierre-Auguste Renoir   58
Paul Cézanne   60
Paul Gauguin   62
Vincent van Gogh   65
Gustav Klimt   68
Henri Matisse   70
Wassily Kandinsky   74
Pablo Picasso   76
Edward Hopper   80
Rene Magritte   82
Salvador Dalí   84
Jackson Pollock   86
Andy Warhol   88
Glossary   90
About the pictures   92
Index   96

About this book

Over the centuries, all kinds of different artists have been admired and celebrated for many different reasons. Some of them have been unappreciated during their own lifetimes, becoming famous only after their deaths. Others have gained notoriety for the way they lived, as much as for their art, while others have shunned publicity, letting their work speak for itself.

This book tells the stories of 35 famous artists, whose work spans hundreds of years and a wide range of styles.

Finding out more

Works by the artists in this book are on display in galleries around the world, and there are museums where you can find out more about how some of them lived and worked.

For links to the museum and gallery websites and online art activities, go to **www.usborne.com/quicklinks** and type in the keywords **Famous Artists**.

Please note, the websites are regularly reviewed and updated, but Usborne Publishing is not responsible for the content of any website other than its own.

Throughout this book, there are speech bubbles quoting some of the artists' ideas about art in their own words.

I dream of painting and then I paint my dream.
(Vincent van Gogh)

Giotto

GIOTTO DI BONDONE

AROUND **1266-1337**

No one knows what Giotto really looked like, as no portraits have survived from his time. This was painted 200 years after his death.

Giotto was a medieval painter who rose to fame in the city of Florence in the late 13th century. He's one of the earliest artists whose life story we know much about, though some details have been lost over time. But many of his paintings have survived, and are still widely admired today.

Giotto may have started life as a shepherd boy. Legend has it that his talent was discovered when a passing artist saw him sketching pictures of his sheep on a rock. Another story tells that, when Giotto was an apprentice painter, he painted a fly on the face of one of his master's portraits. It was so realistic, the master tried to brush it off, thinking it was real.

These stories may not be true, but Giotto was certainly very talented. At the time, most paintings were religious and were often painted in a very stylized, unrealistic way. But Giotto gave his figures solid-looking bodies, expressive faces and dramatic gestures that emphasized their emotions. He was much in demand, working in many cities as well as Florence, including Assisi and Naples.

Around 1266
Giotto di Bondone is born in or near to the city of Florence, in what is now Italy. As a boy, he is thought to have worked as a shepherd.

1297-1300
Around this time he may be working in Florence and Rome, learning from other Italian painters there.

1301
By this time, he probably has a large workshop in Florence.

c.1305
He paints the inside of the Arena Chapel in Padua, with scenes from the lives of Jesus and his mother, Mary.

1306-1311
He probably goes to Assisi to make more wall paintings.

Lasting legacy

As well as making large paintings to hang up in churches, Giotto also painted scenes directly onto the walls of churches and chapels. Later in his life, he was even asked to try his hand at architecture, designing a bell tower for Florence Cathedral. Although he died before it was finished, it was completed by later artists and is still standing today. This building, and the paintings Giotto left behind, are now regarded as some of the most important art treasures in Europe.

The Arena Chapel in Padua, Italy, with wall paintings by Giotto

LAMENTATION OVER THE DEAD CHRIST

Giotto made this wall painting in the Arena Chapel around 1305. It shows the followers of Jesus, and the angels above, mourning over his body.

The Campanile (bell tower) in Florence

1328
He is working for King Robert of Anjou in Naples.

1334
He is asked to design a campanile (bell tower) for Florence Cathedral.

1337
Giotto dies.

Jan van Eyck
1395-1441

Van Eyck was one of the first artists in northern Europe to achieve great success painting with oils. His paintings combine lifelike portraits with glowing light, convincing textures and realistic, detailed landscapes.

PORTRAIT OF A MAN
(thought to be a self portrait)

This is a photograph of the city of Bruges, where van Eyck lived and worked for many years.

Jan van Eyck was born in the city of Maaseik (in what is now Belgium) in 1395. Little is known about his early life, but by his 20s, he was already a hugely successful painter. At this time, oil paints were fairly new, and van Eyck was so good with them that some later experts thought he had invented them. This wasn't true, but he was one of the first to demonstrate the amazing effects that oil painting could achieve.

Because of van Eyck's talent, he was in demand by rich and powerful clients. At the age of 31, he went to work for the Duke of Burgundy in the city of Bruges. But van Eyck also found time to paint for other well-to-do art-lovers, from rich merchants who wanted portraits of themselves, to powerful churchmen who paid for huge religious paintings.

Around 1395
Jan van Eyck is born in the city of Maaseik.

1422-4
By now, he is a court painter to Duke John of Bavaria, based at the Hague in the Netherlands.

1425
When the Duke of Bavaria dies, Jan goes to work for Duke Philip the Good of Burgundy.

1426
Jan moves to the city of Bruges, where he lives for the rest of his life.

Eye for detail

Van Eyck loved detail, and his paintings often feature beautiful patterns, intricate carvings and elaborate architecture.

Although many of his paintings depict Biblical stories, he based the settings closely on the cities and landscapes of the area of the Netherlands where he lived.

Some experts think Jan had a brother, Hubert, and a sister, Margaret, who were artists too.

1426–1432
During this period, Jan works on a huge religious painting for a church in the city of Ghent, in what is now Belgium.

1441
Jan van Eyck dies.

VIRGIN AND CHILD WITH CHANCELLOR ROLIN
This painting was paid for by a rich churchman named Rolin, shown on the left. Opposite are baby Jesus and his mother, the Virgin Mary. Although it looks as if Rolin is in the same room, the other figures are supposed to be in a heavenly scene in his imagination, as he prays to them.

The man in the red hat

Although many paintings by van Eyck survive, not much is known about him as a person. He only left behind one portrait (opposite) that most experts believe to be a picture of himself, but it's possible he painted himself into other pictures. In the painting above, the tiny figure in the middle wearing a red hat may represent van Eyck.

Leonardo da Vinci

Leonardo da Vinci is famous as one of the most gifted artists of all time, and as an imaginative inventor. But he was so busy thinking up new ideas that he often abandoned his paintings before he had finished them. Only around ten finished paintings by him survive today.

Leonardo was born in the village of Vinci near Florence, in what is now Italy. From an early age, he constantly made models and sketches, a habit he kept up for his entire life. But he was restless and found it hard to concentrate on one thing at a time.

SELF PORTRAIT AS AN OLD MAN

This is one of Leonardo's many notebooks, where he made lots of notes and sketched things that interested him. The writing is all reversed and written from right to left, so it's very hard to read. Leonardo may have done this in order to keep his notes secret.

April 15, 1452
Leonardo is born.

1466
He studies painting in Florence with the master painter Verrocchio.

1472
He qualifies as a master painter.

1478
He sets up his own painting workshop, perhaps in Florence.

1482
He moves to Milan and paints several large religious paintings, including *The Last Supper*.

1492
He finishes a huge clay statue of a horse.

10

Starting out

When he was just 14 years old, Leonardo's father sent him to Florence to study with a painter named Verrocchio. Verrocchio was extremely impressed with his young pupil, and there's even a story that he vowed he would never paint again when he saw how talented Leonardo was.

Leonardo soon started out as a painter himself, but it was his many other ideas that brought him to fame. He drew designs for all kinds of things, including water mills, cranes, weapons and flying machines. He was also a talented musician, and it's said he first met the Duke of Milan when he played for him on a silver harp he had designed himself. The Duke was so impressed he immediately asked Leonardo to work for him, and Leonardo soon moved to Milan.

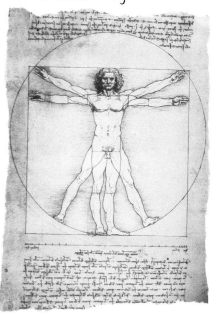

VITRUVIAN MAN

Leonardo was very interested in mathematics. This design shows the mathematical proportions of the human body.

This is a model of a flying machine Leonardo designed. It was never built during his lifetime, and, like many of his inventions, it wouldn't actually have worked.

May 2, 1519
Leonardo dies.

1499 onward
Because of a war, he moves from one city to another working for various powerful noblemen, making paintings and drawing designs for military equipment, including a kind of tank.

1503
He moves to Florence and works on a huge wall painting of a battle scene, and on Mona Lisa.

1508
He moves back to Milan.

from 1513
He moves to Rome and works for the Pope, alongside Michelangelo and Raphael.

1516
He moves to France to work for the French king.

The paint of this famous
painting has flaked so
badly, it's had to be restored
and retouched many times.
To try to preserve it, only
a few visitors at a time
are allowed in to see it.

Getting distracted

Leonardo made several paintings while he was in Milan, including one of the last supper shared by Jesus with his followers, high on a wall inside a monastery building. He painted very slowly, sometimes just staring at his work for hours, which was very frustrating for the monks. Unfortunately, he had coated the wall with an experimental waterproof undercoat, and the paint started to flake off it almost as soon as he had finished.

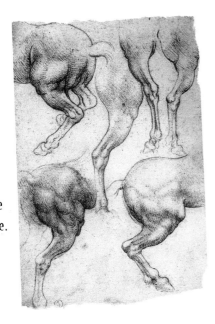

These are some of Leonardo's sketches for his huge horse statue.

While Leonardo was in Milan, he also designed a huge bronze statue of a previous Duke of Milan on a horse. He sculpted a clay version as a trial run, but never got around to making the finished statue. A war swept through the region, and invading troops used the clay statue as a target to fire at, and blew it to pieces.

For the next few years, Leonardo moved from city to city to avoid the fighting. He was always in demand, designing maps, defensive buildings and military equipment.

Disasters and triumphs

Leonardo hadn't given up his painting. He was asked to make a vast wall painting for a room in Florence, showing a fierce battle. After his disaster with *The Last Supper*, he tried a different type of waterproof undercoat, but this time the wet paint dripped right off the wall. He tried to dry the paint quickly using charcoal stoves, but he only managed to save part of the painting.

Around the same time, he completed what must be the most famous painting of all time: *Mona Lisa*. Luckily this time he used traditional methods that lasted well.

MONA LISA

There have been many theories over the years about who the woman in this portrait was. It's now widely accepted that her name was Lisa and that she was married to a man named Francesco del Giocondo, who asked Leonardo to make the painting.

The king's painter

Eventually, like many other artists of the time, Leonardo was called to Rome to work for the Pope, the leader of the Catholic Church. But in 1516 Leonardo had a more attractive offer from the French king and moved to France, where he was given a handsome salary and even his own castle to live in. He died just three years later, and it's said that the king, who had become a close friend, was there himself, comforting the great artist in his final moments.

The King of France said he had actually held Leonardo in his arms as he died.

Albrecht Dürer

1471-1528

Dürer was one of the first artists to become famous throughout Europe in his own lifetime. He made large paintings and black-and-white prints, and filled his work with intricate details copied from nature.

SELF PORTRAIT WITH GLOVES

Albrecht Dürer was born in the German city of Nuremberg. Having trained with a successful painter, he left to travel around Europe, studying the work of other artists and making drawings and watercolors of the different landscapes, plants and animals he saw. When he returned to Nuremberg at the age of 24, he settled down to make his living as an artist.

Dürer used the sketches he had made, putting glimpses of landscapes into the background of some of his paintings, and showing realistic groups of animals, birds and flowers in others. This gave his work a fresh and lifelike look.

View of Nuremberg

May 21, 1471
Durer is born in Nuremberg.

1486
He starts working as an apprentice with Nuremberg painter Michael Wolgemut.

1490-95
He travels around Europe.

1495
He sets up his own workshop in Nuremberg, selling mainly black-and-white prints.

1505-1507
He visits Venice, where he works on large paintings.

14

Printed masterpieces

Although Dürer continued to make delicate watercolor sketches and large, colorful paintings, for most of his life he concentrated on black-and-white prints. These were made by carving wooden blocks or engraving metal plates, which were then inked and pressed onto paper. Although Dürer's prints sold well in the rest of Europe, he was frustrated that it took much longer for his talents to be recognized at home in Nuremberg.

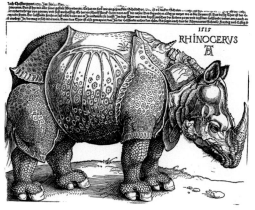

The Rhinoceros
This impressive picture of a rhinoceros is one of Dürer's most famous prints.

A Young Hare
Dürer made this small painting from a live hare, capturing every detail of its fur. He signed it with an arrangement of his initials, AD. Almost all his works have this signature.

Fame at last

As people in other countries got to know of Dürer's work, his fame gradually spread. By the end of his life, he was treated as a celebrity artist wherever he went. Soon after his death, at the age of just 57, people were calling him 'the prince among German painters'.

1507-1509
Back in Nuremberg, he becomes increasingly well-known. He works on more paintings and prints.

from 1525
He works on books about art with illustrations showing things such as drawing machines like the one on the right — the artist peers through a viewfinder and traces what he sees onto a pane of glass.

1515
He starts working for the powerful Emperor Maximilian I.

Viewfinder

Pane of glass

April 6, 1528
He dies.

Michelangelo

MICHELANGELO BUONARROTI
1475–1564

Michelangelo was an astonishingly talented man. As well as being one of the greatest sculptors of all time, he was also an amazingly gifted painter, architect, and poet. But even his friends complained that he was grumpy, smelly, and hated being around other people.

DAVID

This is Michelangelo's most famous work, a nude statue of the Bible character David.

Michelangelo was born in a small village near Florence, in what is now Italy. He started as an apprentice painter at 13 years old, but soon switched to sculpture. By the age of 20, he had carved a statue in an ancient Roman style that looked so convincing it was sold as a genuine antique.

Word of his talent and energy soon spread, and some Florentine officials asked him to carve a statue from a vast, awkwardly shaped block of marble. The finished statue, *David*, was so graceful, the city of Florence adopted it as their mascot.

Michelangelo made this sketch when he was working on his statue. David holds a sling in his raised hand. In the Bible, David used this to kill a giant named Goliath.

March 6, 1475
Michelangelo is born in the village of Caprese, near Florence.

1488
He starts working as an apprentice painter.

1490–92
He studies sculpture at an academy founded by an important politician, Lorenzo de Medici, in Florence.

1494–5
He carves a Roman-style sculpture so convincing, it's sold as an antique.

The Holy Family

This painting shows the baby Jesus with his mother Mary and his father Joseph.

Michelangelo added Jesus's cousin, St. John, further back, and a row of nude male figures behind the holy family. These were inspired by ancient Roman statues.

Michelangelo was fascinated by how the human body worked, and drew from live models, even though people strongly disapproved.

In demand

By now, Michelangelo had lots of wealthy art-lovers in Florence and Rome willing to pay for his work, so he divided his time between these two great Italian cities, and between sculpture and painting. By 1503, Michelangelo's talent had been noted by the Pope, and he was called to Rome to work for him, perhaps the most prestigious position for an artist then.

1504
He finishes carving *David* from a vast block of marble.

1508-1512
He paints the ceiling of the Sistine Chapel in Rome.

1530
He paints *The Last Judgement* on the end wall of the Sistine Chapel.

1546
He is appointed as architect for St. Peter's Basilica in Rome.

February 18, 1564
He dies in Rome at the age of 88.

THE SISTINE CHAPEL
This ceiling contains over 300 figures telling different stories from the Bible. These are arranged in scenes, with nude figures in between them.

Many talents

Michelangelo had become so famous that the Pope asked him to decorate the ceiling of a huge chapel in his residence in Rome. As well as making the painting, Michelangelo had to invent a system of scaffolding so that his painting platform wouldn't leave holes in the ceiling. It took him around four years to complete the painting. Then, the next Pope asked him to decorate the end wall of the chapel with another huge painting, *The Last Judgement*.

Michelangelo had to work at a back-breaking angle to paint the ceiling of the Sistine Chapel. He even wrote poems complaining about how uncomfortable it was.

Michelangelo was a talented architect, too, designing a dome to span the vast church of St. Peter's in Rome. Sadly, he only managed to plan the dome before he died at the age of 88, still working as hard as ever. But it was completed around 50 years later, and it's been the tallest dome in the world ever since.

Raphael

Raphael was the son of a successful Italian painter, but he far outstripped his father to become one of the most famous painters of his day, holding his own against outstanding artists such as Michelangelo and Leonardo da Vinci.

SELF PORTRAIT
Raphael painted this picture when he was around 20.

Raphael's father, a painter named Giovanni Santi, worked for the Duke of Urbino. Giovanni died when Raphael was only 11 years old, but by this time, the boy's artistic talent was obvious. It's thought he may have gone on to study with a painter named Perugino. By the age of 17, Raphael was working as a painter.

The house in Urbino where it's thought Raphael was born

Close to home

For the next few years, Raphael worked on religious paintings for churches near Urbino, and on paintings of ancient myths or portraits for wealthy members of the Duke of Urbino's court. Then, at the age of just 21, he was invited to make paintings in other Italian towns, including Florence, a city packed with amazingly talented artists.

Raphael is famous for drawing and painting charming baby angels, like this one. They are sometimes known as cherubs, or putti.

19

Florence and Rome

Raphael was very quick to pick up new ideas and techniques. In Florence, he met and learned from many artists including Leonardo da Vinci. Soon, he was called to Rome to work for the Pope alongside artists including Michelangelo. But they argued, as Michelangelo was jealous of Raphael's early success, and claimed that Raphael had stolen his ideas.

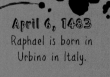

Raphael was multi-talented and worked on many different projects at once, designing tapestries and buildings as well as making paintings.

ST. GEORGE AND THE DRAGON

This painting shows St. George killing a fearsome dragon in order to rescue a maiden. You can see her in the background.

Raphael made several paintings of St. George and the dragon. This one was painted in 1504.

April 6, 1483
Raphael is born in Urbino in Italy.

1494
His father dies.

1500
Raphael qualifies as a master painter.

c.1502-3
He works near Urbino on paintings for churches and wealthy people.

The Alba Madonna

This painting, showing the baby Jesus with his mother Mary (known as the Madonna) and his small cousin, St. John, behind him, was made for a wealthy churchman. It was later owned by a family named Alba, whose name is now part of the painting's title.

Raphael made many paintings of the Madonna throughout his life.

Final years

In Rome, Raphael went from strength to strength, developing his own distinctive style, but also incorporating many new ideas inspired by other artists. Like all artists at this time, Raphael employed lots of assistants, so he produced paintings very quickly, not only for the Pope, but for other rich and powerful clients as well. But, at the age of only 37, Raphael was struck down by a fever and, tragically, died.

Raphael didn't actually copy Michelangelo, but he was fascinated by his work. He's supposed to have persuaded an influential friend to let him in to see Michelangelo's Sistine Chapel ceiling, before it was officially unveiled.

1504-8
He spends time in Florence and studies the works of Leonardo and Michelangelo.

1508
He moves to Rome to work for the Pope. He starts work on wall paintings to decorate the Pope's private library.

1511-12
He designs and paints more rooms for the Pope's weekend retreat outside Rome.

1515-16
He designs a set of tapestries for the Sistine Chapel.

1520
He dies from a fever in Rome.

21

Titian

Tiziano Vecellio
AROUND 1488–1576

SELF PORTRAIT

Titian painted everything from portraits and nude women to dramatic action scenes. His talent so outshone other artists of his day, they called him 'the Sun among small stars'.

FLORA

Titian often painted beautiful women with reddish-gold hair. This one is dressed as the Roman flower goddess, Flora.

Titian's career started early. He was probably around 12 years old when he went to study painting in the Italian city of Venice with a leading artist, Gentile Bellini.

Gentile didn't get on with Titian – he thought he painted too quickly. So Titian went to work for Gentile's brother Giovanni, another top Venetian painter. Titian learned much from Giovanni and, by the age of 22, he left Venice to try his luck as a solo artist. After three years he came back full of confidence, and asked to be appointed as Venice's official artist, a position held by his old teacher Giovanni Bellini. When Giovanni died three years later, Titian's bold request was granted.

Art is stronger than nature.

around 1488
Born in the city of Pieve de Cadore, near Venice in Italy.

1500
Studies with Gentile Bellini; then with Gentile's brother, Giovanni.

1510
Moves to Padua where he works on a series of wall paintings.

1513
Returns to Venice. Offers to paint a battle scene and in return, asks for the 'senseria' (appointment as official painter for Venice).

22

Bacchus and Ariadne

This painting shows a scene from an ancient Greek myth. The woman on the far left is Ariadne, a heroine who has been deserted by the man she loved.

The central figure with the pink drapery is the god Bacchus, who has come to rescue her. The other figures are followers of Bacchus.

Troubled times

Titian continued to make large, dramatic paintings, but as his fame spread he was asked to paint portraits of the rich and powerful: politicians, dukes, princes, a pope and even an emperor. Despite great success and vast wealth, Titian continued to work as hard as ever, often going back to his paintings over and over again for years, never satisfied with his work.

Titian was around 80 when a terrible plague spread to Venice. He was just one of thousands who died, but he was so famous and well respected, he was the only one given a proper burial service.

December 1576
Titian dies of the plague.

1556
He is elected to the Florentine academy of painters.

1545-6
He visits Rome where he begins a series of portraits. He is given Roman citizenship.

1516
On the death of Giovanni Bellini, Titian takes over as the official state painter of Venice.

1525
He marries, but his wife dies in childbirth in 1530.

1533
He receives a knighthood from Charles V, the Holy Roman Emperor, and becomes his official court painter.

Hans Holbein

Hans Holbein the Younger
1497/98–1543

Self **P**ortrait

Hans Holbein's vivid, lifelike portraits made him one of the most celebrated artists of the 16th century. He painted some of the most famous men of his day, including Henry VIII, the King of England.

This engraving of Hans as a boy (right) and his brother Ambrosius was made by their father.

Growing up in Augsburg, in what is now southern Germany, Holbein came from a family of artists – both his father and his brother were painters.

As a young artist, Holbein designed stained glass and made woodcut prints, as well as painting pictures and making his first portraits. These were of the philosopher Erasmus, who became his friend. They were so true to life, they made Holbein's reputation.

Then, seeking new inspiration, Holbein set out for England. In London, he found powerful patrons, and after returning home for four years, he settled in England for good. He soon attracted rich clients with his lavish portraits, such as *The Ambassadors*.

1497 or 98
Born in Augsburg, in what is now southern Germany.

1515
Moves to Basel, Switzerland, with his brother Ambrosius. When his brother dies, he takes over his workshop.

1523
Paints three portraits of the philosopher Erasmus.

1526
Travels to England. Makes portraits of Thomas More and his family, before returning home.

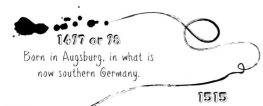

1532
Returns to England, leaving his wife and two children behind.

1535
Designs the title page for the first complete Bible printed in English.

November 1543
Dies, in London, probably of the plague.

from 1536
Works as Henry VIII's court painter.

Images of power

At the age of 39, Holbein came to the attention of the most powerful man in England – King Henry VIII. Henry wanted to create an image of himself as ruthless, aggressive and powerful, and Holbein's portraits of him did just that.

Then, in 1536, Henry was looking for a new wife, and sent Holbein to paint his possible brides. Henry was impressed by Holbein's flattering portrait of Anne of Cleves, and chose her, but when they met, he was disappointed. Holbein received few royal commissions after that – but he didn't entirely lose Henry's favor. When he died, at the young age of 45, he was working on a portrait of the King.

This is a design Holbein made for a gold cup. At Henry's court, Holbein also designed jewels, weapons and other items of metalwork.

THE AMBASSADORS
One of Holbein's most famous paintings, this shows two powerful young men, surrounded by symbols of wealth and learning. In front of them is a distorted skull – a reminder of death. You can see it more clearly if you shut one eye and look at it from the side.

Bruegel

PIETER BRUEGEL THE ELDER
AROUND 1525-1569

This drawing of an artist by Bruegel may be a self portrait.

Painting ran in Pieter Bruegel's family. He had two sons (one of them also called Pieter) who became painters, too. The first Pieter Bruegel is known as 'the Elder', to tell him apart from his son. He's famous for his lively outdoor scenes, crowded with people.

Bruegel may have dressed up as a peasant so he could mix unnoticed at country dances.

Bruegel was born in the Netherlands. He trained with a successful painter in the town of Antwerp, and then developed his skills visiting Lyons in France, and Italian cities including Naples and Rome. When he came back, he settled in Antwerp and started painting and drawing everything from religious stories to ancient Greek legends and strange imaginary scenes. But he was always inspired by his surroundings, and painted people, houses and landscapes similar to those he saw around him. Apparently, he even went in disguise to village celebrations, to collect ideas for local costumes and other details to include in his paintings.

BIG FISH EAT LITTLE FISH

As well as making large paintings, Bruegel also made drawings, which were made into black-and-white prints, like this one.

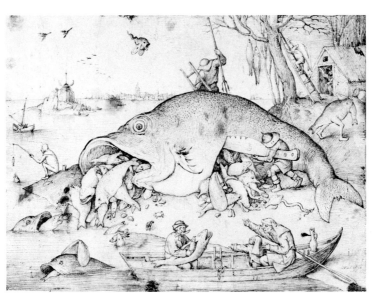

This monstrous fish has smaller fish spilling out of its body. Bruegel created several disturbing, dreamlike scenes like this one. Even so, many of the details are copied from real life.

Around 1525
Pieter Bruegel is born in Breda in the Netherlands.

1551
He becomes a professional painter in the prosperous town of Antwerp.

Settling down

When Bruegel was in his late thirties, he moved to Brussels and married Mayken, the daughter of his old teacher. By this time he was a successful artist, and his works were being bought by powerful churchmen and rich bankers. The City Council of Brussels even asked him to paint several pictures to celebrate the building of a new canal between Antwerp and Brussels.

This photograph shows part of Brussels, where Bruegel lived in later life.

WINTER LANDSCAPE WITH SKATERS AND A BIRD TRAP
This painting shows people skating on a frozen river in a wintry setting. The bird trap is the flat wooden structure you can see under the largest tree.

Bruegel died when he was around 44. His sons were only small children, so it's unlikely he taught them to paint himself. But it was probably his lively work that led them to becoming painters when they grew up.

September 9, 1569
Pieter Bruegel dies.

1568
He has a second son named Jan, who also becomes a painter.

1564
He has a son named Pieter who eventually becomes a painter, known as Pieter Bruegel the Younger.

1563
He moves to Brussels.

1555–63
He returns to Antwerp.

1552–4
He travels to Lyons, Naples and Rome, among other places, learning about art and painting.

27

El Greco

DOMÉNIKOS THEOTOKÓPOULOS
1541–1614

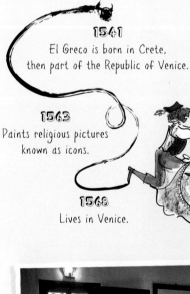

PORTRAIT OF AN OLD MAN
This is probably a self portrait.

El Greco painted in a very unusual style, creating elongated figures and using intense colors to create dramatic religious scenes.

El Greco, or 'the Greek', was the nickname of the artist Doménikos Theotokópoulos. He grew up on the island of Crete, where he studied painting in a monastery. As a young man, he left Crete, and by 1572 he was living in Rome, the center of European art, where he opened a workshop.

No one knows why for sure, but within a few years El Greco had left for Spain. It is reported that he was hounded out of Rome for saying that Michelangelo, the city's most famous painter, 'did not know how to paint.' He had even offered to paint over *The Last Judgment*, one of Michelangelo's most famous works.

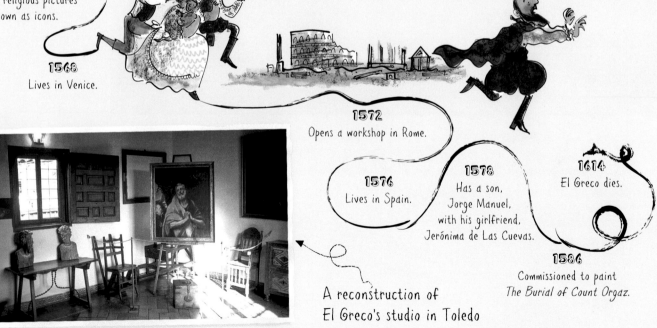

1541
El Greco is born in Crete, then part of the Republic of Venice.

1563
Paints religious pictures known as icons.

1568
Lives in Venice.

1572
Opens a workshop in Rome.

1576
Lives in Spain.

1578
Has a son, Jorge Manuel, with his girlfriend, Jerónima de Las Cuevas.

1614
El Greco dies.

1586
Commissioned to paint *The Burial of Count Orgaz.*

A reconstruction of El Greco's studio in Toledo

In Toledo

In Spain, El Greco hoped to become a court painter to King Philip II, and won a commission for two major works. But the King didn't like them, probably because of El Greco's unusual style. The paintings had raw, bright colors and included strange, distorted figures. The King never commissioned El Greco again.

El Greco settled in the city of Toledo, where he spent the rest of his life. He became a great success, and wrote on art, sculpture and philosophy, as well as painting.

The city of Toledo, where El Greco made his home

A forgotten fool?

After El Greco's death, his art was largely forgotten. He gained a reputation as eccentric, foolish and even insane. It wasn't until the 19th century that people rediscovered his work. Since then, El Greco has inspired many different artists, including Manet, Cézanne and Picasso.

THE BURIAL OF COUNT ORGAZ

This is one of El Greco's most famous paintings. According to a legend, the Count was a very holy man. When he died, two saints descended from Heaven to help with his burial. The young boy in the bottom left-hand corner is El Greco's son, Jorge Manuel.

29

Caravaggio

MICHELANGELO MERISI DI CARAVAGGIO
1571-1610

Portrait by Ottavio Leoni

Caravaggio was the most influential and controversial Italian painter of the 17th century. His paintings were often shockingly realistic, and made dramatic use of light and shade. His life was dramatic too – he killed a man and spent the rest of his life on the run.

Michelangelo Merisi was born in Milan and grew up in nearby Caravaggio. Little is known about his childhood, but when he was 21 he moved to Rome, in search of fame and fortune as an artist.

Calling himself Caravaggio, after the village he came from, he started out painting still lifes to sell in the streets. But his big break came in 1599, when he won the first of several contracts for large religious paintings to decorate churches.

THE BASKET OF FRUIT
This still life painting is so realistic, there's even a maggot hole in the apple.

Caravaggio soon became known as 'the most famous painter in Rome' – as much for his violent temper as for his talent. He was arrested several times for brawling. Then, in 1606, he killed a man in a fight, apparently after losing a tennis match.

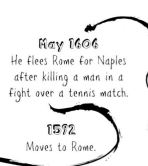

May 1606
He flees Rome for Naples after killing a man in a fight over a tennis match.

1572
Moves to Rome.

September 29, 1571
Michelangelo Merisi is born in Milan.

1584-88
He is apprenticed to a painter in Milan.

Artist in exile

Rather than face punishment by the authorities in Rome, Caravaggio went on the run. He fled to Naples, moving on to Malta, then to Sicily. He produced many great paintings along the way, but he always longed to return to Rome.

In 1610, he set sail on a small boat heading for Rome, in the hope that influential friends could persuade the Roman authorities to grant him a pardon so that he could return home.

The pardon was granted, but Caravaggio never made it back. His boat stopped off at the Italian port of Porto Ercole, then sailed off again without him, carrying all his belongings away. Exhausted, broke and alone, Caravaggio collapsed with a fever and died.

July 18, 1610
Caravaggio catches a
fever at Porto Ercole
and dies at 38.

1610
Sets sail
for Rome.

October 1609
Returns to Naples.

1609
Paints alterpieces for
three churches in Sicily.

October 1606
He settles in Naples.

July 1607
He moves to Malta, where he makes
paintings for the Knights of St. John.

July 1608
Made a Knight
of St. John.

December 1608
Gets into a fight; leaves Malta in disgrace.

Peter Paul Rubens

1577-1640

Rubens painted this self portrait when he was 41.

A brilliant scholar and a diplomat, Rubens was also one of the most prolific artists of the 17th century. His paintings were bold, busy and extravagant — as was his life.

Rubens was born in Siegen, in what is now Germany. His family moved to Antwerp when he was 12, and a year later, Rubens began to work as an apprentice painter. At 22, he set out on a journey to Venice, where he saw works by many great artists, including Titian. The trip inspired him so much that, from that moment on, he signed his name in Italian – 'Pietro Paulo Rubens'.

Rubens settled in the Italian city of Mantua, where he became the court painter to Vincenzo I Gonzaga, the Duke of Mantua. Gonzaga was so impressed with Rubens that he also employed him as a diplomat, sending him to Spain with gifts for King Philip III. On the way, two works of art were damaged in a rainstorm, but Rubens quickly painted replacements.

My talent is such, that no undertaking however vast in size... has ever surpassed my courage.

In Rome, Rubens was inspired by antique statues.

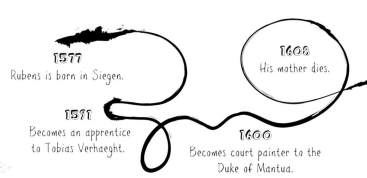

1577
Rubens is born in Siegen.

1591
Becomes an apprentice to Tobias Verhaeght.

1600
Becomes court painter to the Duke of Mantua.

1608
His mother dies.

SELF PORTRAIT WITH ISABELLA BRANT

Rubens painted this portrait of himself and his wife in 1609, the year they were married. He said that his wife was 'all goodness and honesty'.

Returning home

In October 1608, Rubens received news that his mother was seriously ill. He rushed home to Antwerp, but by the time he arrived, she had already died. The Prince Regent persuaded him to stay, by offering him the post of court painter.

By now Rubens was attracting lots of pupils, and he was soon in charge of an enormous workshop. As the commissions rolled in, he often got his assistants to begin his paintings, while he finished off the details.

He worked with incredible energy, waking up at four every morning to go to church before work. One visitor to his studio described the artist listening to a poetry recital, directing his assistants and painting a canvas, all at the same time.

This sketch by Rubens is thought to be of his and Isabella's son Nicolas.

An artist abroad

In 1626, Rubens's wife died. He was devastated, and threw himself into his work, going on diplomatic missions to Spain and England, where King Charles I commissioned a series of paintings for his Banqueting House in London.

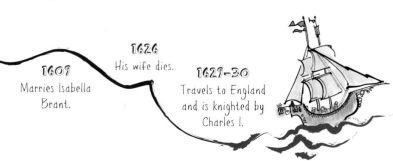

1609
Marries Isabella Brant.

1626
His wife dies.

1627–30
Travels to England and is knighted by Charles I.

1630
Marries Hélène Fourment. They go on to have two sons and three daughters.

Rubens included a self portrait in this scene. He's the one with the beard, below the musicians, gazing out of the picture.

A second family

In 1630, Rubens was married again, to 16-year-old Hélène Fourment. They had four children together, and Rubens was devoted to them. The family moved to a grand house in the countryside where Rubens planned to spend less time working.

But his paintings were still in demand. He was working on a series of 120 paintings, and Hélène was expecting their fifth child, when he fell ill, and died.

Marie de Medici, the mother of the King of France, commissioned Rubens to paint 25 enormous paintings celebrating her life. This one shows her coronation.

1635
Buys a large country house, the Château Steen. Spends time there with his family and takes up landscape painting.

1635
Begins work on a huge commission of 120 paintings on mythological themes for Philip IV of Spain.

1640
Dies in Antwerp. Eight months later, his last child is born.

Rembrandt

Rembrandt Harmenszoon van Rijn
1606-1669

A miller's son from Leiden, Rembrandt was the most successful Dutch artist of his time, best known for his powerful portraits. But while his career flourished, his home life was clouded by tragedy and bankruptcy, and he died almost penniless.

Self Portrait
Rembrandt made over 90 self portraits, including paintings and prints. This one was painted when he was 23.

Little is known about Rembrandt's childhood, but he must have been clever. He was one of nine children, and while his brothers were sent to learn trades, Rembrandt went to grammar school and then started university.

However, academic life wasn't for him. He left university and became a painter's apprentice, before setting himself up as an artist. By his early 20s, he had already built himself a strong reputation in Leiden.

But Rembrandt had greater ambitions. So, in 1631, he moved to Amsterdam. It was one of the most prosperous cities in Europe, full of wealthy merchants and exciting opportunities for a young artist eager to make his name.

This painting, by Jacob van der Ulft, shows what central Amsterdam looked like in Rembrandt's time.

Fame and family

Rembrandt moved into the home of an art dealer named Hendrick van Uylenburgh, and married his landlord's cousin, Saskia. It was a happy marriage. Rembrandt made numerous tender sketches of Saskia at home, and she appears in many of his paintings too.

Meanwhile, Rembrandt's career took off. He painted portraits for rich families and organizations, as well as stories from history, mythology and the Bible. These were created with thick, bumpy paint, known as 'impasto', and made dramatic use of light and shade.

This is a chalk drawing of Rembrandt's wife Saskia and their first child. They had four children, but only one survived infancy.

THE NIGHT WATCH

Rather than showing them in a formal pose, Rembrandt painted the soldiers in this group portrait as though they were about to march into action.

July 15, 1606
Rembrandt Harmenszoon van Rijn is born in Leiden, the son of a miller.

1620-23
Becomes an artist's apprentice.

1624
Sets up an art studio in Leiden.

1625
Studies art for six months in Amsterdam.

1631
Moves to Amsterdam

1634
Marries Saskia van Uylenburgh.

1639
Buys a grand house in Jodenbreestraat, Amsterdam.

September, 1641
A son, Titus, is born.

June, 1642
Saskia dies.

Changing fortunes

With the money pouring in, Rembrandt and Saskia bought a grand house, which he filled with art and curios – from Roman busts, costumes and weapons to stuffed birds. In 1641, Saskia gave birth to a son, Titus, but she became unwell, and died the following year. She left her fortune to Rembrandt and Titus, but according to her will, Rembrandt would lose his share if he remarried.

Single life didn't suit him. By 1648, he had fallen in love with a servant named Hendrickje Stoffels. He painted her many times, but he couldn't afford to give up his inheritance to marry her.

Rembrandt drew himself making all kinds of faces so he could practice portraying different emotions.

SELF PORTRAIT AT THE AGE OF **63**
Made the year he died, this is one of Rembrandt's very last paintings.

Money woes

In the 1650s, Amsterdam was hit by a financial crash, and Rembrandt wasn't earning as much as before. Unable to make the payments on his house, he was declared insolvent and his belongings were sold off to pay his debts.

Hendrickje died in 1663, followed by Titus five years later. Despite the bereavements, and continuing debts, the 1660s was a prolific period for Rembrandt and he kept painting until he died.

by 1648
Hendrickje Stoffels has become his mistress.

1654
A daughter, Cornelia, is born to Hendrickje.

1656
Declared insolvent. His collections are later sold to pay his debts.

October 4, 1669
Rembrandt dies.

1663
Hendrickje dies.

1668
Titus dies.

Diego Velázquez
1599-1660

As a young man, Diego Velázquez wanted to be a great artist, and to be respected for it. In Spain, most people saw painting as a lowly craft. But Velázquez was determined to prove that it could be a noble art.

Velázquez included this self portrait in *The Maids of Honor*.

THE MAIDS OF HONOR
This painting by Velázquez shows Philip IV's daughter, the Infanta Margarita, surrounded by courtiers.

Velázquez grew up in Seville, in Spain, and began to study painting when he was only 10. He became an apprentice to the artist Francisco Pacheco, and by the time he was 18 he had astonished his teacher with his talent, and married his teacher's daughter, Juana.

He was fast making a reputation as a painter of amazingly realistic scenes. Then, in 1623, he was asked to paint King Philip IV. Philip was so impressed by the portrait that he made Velázquez his official painter.

Velázquez painted *The Maids of Honor* before he was knighted. Philip IV is thought to have added in Velázquez's red cross, the sign of the Order of Santiago, after Velázquez had died.

38

At the Royal Court

As a painter at Philip's court, Velázquez only received the same allowance as the royal barber – but he was determined to advance his career. He rose through the court, eventually becoming Chamberlain to the Royal Household, in charge of organizing ceremonies, and many other household tasks. His post only had one drawback – his duties left him hardly any time to paint.

PORTRAIT OF POPE INNOCENT X

This portrait of Pope Innocent made him look so ruthless, many thought the Pope would disapprove of it. Instead, he hung it in his waiting room.

1599
Diego Velázquez is born in Seville, the richest city in Spain.

1609
Begins his training, under Francisco de Herrera, known as a 'pitiless man'. He soon becomes apprentice to Francisco Pacheco instead.

1617
Sets up his own workshop

April 23, 1618
Marries Juana Pacheco.

1623
Philip IV appoints Velázquez as his 'chamber painter'.

1628
Shares a studio with Rubens.

1649
Visits Italy.

1656
Paints *The Maids of Honor.*

1659
Becomes a Knight of the Order of Santiago.

1660
Velázquez dies of a fever. Eight days later, his wife dies.

As Philip IV grew older, he no longer wanted to be painted – he said that he didn't want a record of himself looking old. But he was very fond of Velázquez, and fulfilled his wish to become part of the nobility, making him a Knight of the Order of Santiago.

A year later, Velasquez was in charge of the decorations for the lavish wedding of Philip's daughter. Afterwards, the exhausted artist caught a fever and died. Philip missed him terribly, writing: 'I am crushed.'

Jan Vermeer

Joannis Reijniersz Vermeer

1632-1675

This figure from one of Vermeer's paintings may be meant as a self portrait. If so, it's the only portrait of Vermeer that survives.

Vermeer is now one of the most famous artists in the world. But he was not a great success in his own lifetime. His detailed, delicate paintings of domestic life didn't come to fame until 200 years after his death.

Vermeer was born in the city of Delft in the Netherlands, and lived there all his life. At the age of 20, he took over his father's business as an art dealer, and became an artist at around the same time. His studio was in a room at the front of his house, on the second floor. He shut himself up there to paint, setting up lots of props and assistants in costume to create detailed scenes, and then copying them very carefully.

VIEW OF DELFT

Vermeer only painted a very few outdoor scenes. This one shows his home city which by Vermeer's time had become famous for making and exporting decorative blue and white china.

1632
Jan Vermeer is born in the city of Delft, in the Netherlands.

1652
His father dies. Jan takes over the family business as an art dealer.

1653
He becomes a member of the Guild of St. Luke, which means he is now a professional painter.

The Artist's Studio

In this painting Vermeer may be hinting at how he worked. He shows an artist at an easel, painting a costumed figure surrounded by props. But this scene may be misleading.

Some experts think Vermeer used an early type of camera, called a camera obscura, when sketching his scenes. He would have sat in a darkened cubicle at the end of his studio. Light from the scene passed through a small hole onto the canvas, where it cast an upside-down image.

Troubled times

Vermeer never made much from his art, or from his art dealing business. He seems to have been reluctant to part with his paintings, but he also lived at a difficult time for artists. Religious disputes, wars, plagues and other disasters – including an explosion that destroyed much of Delft – all made it hard for painters to find people with spare money to spend on art. When Vermeer died, at the age of just 43, it may have been money worries that brought on his final illness.

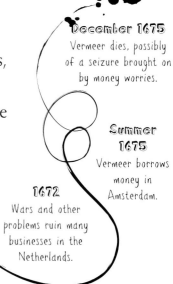

December 1675
Vermeer dies, possibly of a seizure brought on by money worries.

Summer 1675
Vermeer borrows money in Amsterdam.

1672
Wars and other problems ruin many businesses in the Netherlands.

1662
Vermeer becomes the head of the Guild of St. Luke, a sign that local painters respect his work.

1654
A gunpowder store in Delft explodes, destroying much of the city.

Goya

FRANCISCO JOSÉ DE GOYA Y LUCIENTES
1746-1828

SELF PORTRAIT WITH GLASSES

The greatest Spanish artist of the 18th and 19th centuries, Goya lived through a period of social and political upheaval. He endured personal turmoil too, and he recorded all of this in his increasingly nightmarish paintings and prints.

THE SLEEP OF REASON PRODUCES MONSTERS

This is one of a series of 82 prints of monstrous visions entitled 'Los Caprichos' – meaning Follies. It shows Goya asleep at his desk surrounded by the ghoulish creatures of his imagination.

Originally from a small village, Goya's family moved to the city of Zaragoza when he was 14, and he was apprenticed to a local painter. At 18, he moved to Madrid, hoping to make his name.

As his talents became recognized, he was commissioned to paint portraits for wealthy patrons, and eventually he was made an official painter to the Spanish royal family.

Things seemed to be going well, but, at the age of 47, Goya suffered by an illness that nearly killed him, and left him deaf. He became withdrawn, and started making dark and disturbing pictures of fantastical creatures.

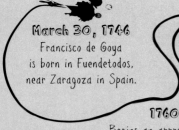

March 30, 1746
Francisco de Goya is born in Fuendetodos, near Zaragoza in Spain.

1760
Begins an apprenticeship with a painter in Zaragoza.

1764
Moves to Madrid.

1771
Paints frescoes for the Pilar Cathedral in Zaragoza.

1773
Marries Josepha Bayeu.

1774
Helps to design tapestries for King Charles III's palace.

1778
Makes a series of etchings based on paintings by Velázquez.

1786
Becomes an official painter to the Spanish royal family.

Dark times

In 1808, French forces invaded Spain and the royal family went into hiding. Six years of war followed. Appalled by the violence and brutality he saw committed on both sides, Goya started making prints and paintings of the horrors of war.

Goya often worked late into the night to finish a painting. He even fixed candles to the brim of his hat to provide extra light while he worked.

THE THIRD OF MAY 1808

This powerful painting records some of the violence Goya witnessed in Madrid after the French invaded Spain.

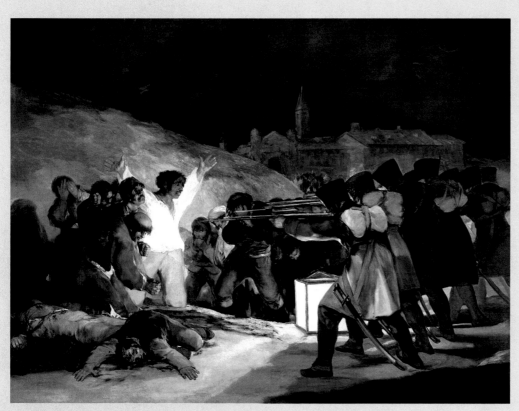

After the war, Goya moved to a house in the country, called 'the House of the Deaf Man' after the previous occupant who had been deaf too. He painted gloomy scenes on the walls – known as the 'Black Paintings' – of hideous monsters and witches.

But life in Spain had changed. Artists and writers were being censored, and universities were being shut down. Goya, now old and weak, sought refuge in France, where he died, age 82.

April 16, 1828
Goya dies in Bordeaux, France, age 82.

1823
Fearing persecution, he leaves Spain for France.

1820–22
Spends most of his time painting 'the Black Paintings' on the walls of his house.

1793
A long illness leaves him deaf.

1799
Publishes 'Los Caprichos' – Follies.

1808
France invades Spain.

1818
Produces a series of prints of bullfighting.

J.M.W. Turner

JOSEPH MALLORD WILLIAM TURNER
1775-1851

This portrait accentuates Turner's distinctive face. According to one friend, he had a projecting chin and a parrot's nose.

A working-class boy from London, Turner grew up to be the most celebrated painter in England. Working ceaselessly for 60 years, he created more than 500 paintings, and 19,000 drawings and sketches.

As a child, Turner sketched people on the streets, and his father, who was a barber, sold these drawings in his barber shop. At the age of 15, Turner became a student at the Royal Academy, and soon after that, he started painting the scenes for a theater. As a young man, he became known for being solitary, silent, and totally devoted to drawing.

This is one of Turner's sketchbooks. The pencil sketch is upside-down. That's because he filled all the right-hand pages first, then flipped the book over so he could work through it again.

Turner liked the element of chance in a picture. He asked children to dip their hands in paint and pat paper to make a pattern – which he then turned into a painting.

Turner's Gallery

By the time he was 30, Turner had opened his own gallery to show his oil paintings and watercolors. At first, it was a great success. But, over the years, it became dusty and neglected, and one visitor reported being, 'alarmed by a multitude of cats'. Turner even used one of his own paintings as a cat flap.

April 23, 1775
Turner is born.

1791
Paints his first oil paintings.

1792
Spends the summer walking and sketching in Wales.

1798
His mother is sent to an insane asylum

1800
Is elected to the Royal Academy, age 24.

1804
Opens his own gallery, three days after the death of his mother.

1807
Becomes a Professor at the Royal Academy. One student remembered that what he usually got from him was, 'a poke in the side, and a grunt.'

1819
Visits Italy, and is inspired by the landscape and art.

1827
Begins a secret relationship with Sophia Caroline Booth.

1829
Turner's father dies. Turner says he feels as if he has 'lost an only child'.

1846
Moves to Chelsea, where he lives with Sophia. He keeps his address a secret. Locals know him only as 'Admiral Booth'.

November 19, 1851
Turner dies. His last words were reported to be, 'the sun is God'.

An eccentric man

As he grew older, Turner gained a reputation for eccentricity. He sometimes finished his paintings after they had been hung on gallery walls. His painting style grew bolder, and surprised even his most devoted fans. When he showed his painting *Snow Storm*, a scene of a ship in stormy seas, critics described it as, 'soap-suds and whitewash'. Turner is reported to have replied, 'What do they think the sea is like? I wish they'd been in it'.

In his last years, Turner became reluctant to sell his paintings. He was fond of them, he called them his 'family'. In his will, he asked for them all to be displayed in a public gallery – as they are today.

THE FIGHTING TEMERAIRE
Turner was very fond of this painting of an old sailing ship being tugged away for scrap. He called it his 'darling' and refused to sell it.

Eugène Delacroix

1798–1863

One of the most famous painters in 19th century France, Delacroix was a man of contradictions. His paintings were full of passion and violence – but the artist himself was charming, scholarly and polite.

Delacroix was known for his elegant appearance. This caricature of him was drawn by Eugène Giraud.

Delacroix's life was full of drama from the start. 'By the age of three,' wrote his friend Alexandre Dumas, 'he had been... burned, drowned, poisoned and choked.' He was burned when a mosquito net caught fire above his bed, drowned when a servant accidentally dropped him into a harbor, poisoned when he ate some rust, and choked when he swallowed a grape.

School life was less exciting, and when he was 16, he signed up as an art student in Paris. At 24, he exhibited his first painting – *The Barque of Dante*. It was a great success, and was bought by the French government.

LIBERTY LEADING THE PEOPLE

Delacroix made this painting to celebrate the July revolution of 1830. Although he did not fight, he believed he had done his duty for his country by painting.

A dramatic spirit

Delacroix was influenced by poets of the time, such as Byron, who wrote about strong emotions, and the wild beauty of the natural world. Byron's poetry inspired Delacroix to paint dramatic scenes, and although critics were sometimes horrified by his more violent paintings, commissions kept rolling in. Some people suspected that someone powerful was secretly helping his career.

According to some stories, Delacroix was the illegitimate son of a powerful statesman, Talleyrand. Whether or not this was true, Delacroix did receive lots of help from the government, and in 1832, he was offered a place on an official trip to Morocco. He painted the landscape of North Africa many times over the next 20 years.

This is a page from a sketchbook Delacroix kept during his visit to Morocco.

As he grew older, Delacroix worked on several large public projects, but his art was falling out of fashion. When he completed his final commission, no one seemed to notice. Bitterly disappointed, Delacroix fell ill, and on August 13, 1863, he died. But within a few years, his bright colors and expressive brushstrokes were inspiring a new generation of artists – the Impressionists.

April 8, 1798
Ferdinand Victor Eugène Delacroix is born in Paris.

1816
Enrolls in Ecole des Beaux-Arts in Paris.

1822
Inspired by the dramatic paintings of another student, Théodore Géricault, Delacroix paints the The Barque of Dante.

One must be bold to extremity: without daring, and even extreme daring, there is no beauty.

1832
Visits North Africa for six months.

1833
Begins first large state commission, the Salon du Roi, in the Bourbon Palace.

August 13, 1863
Dies in Paris.

John Everett Millais

1829-1896

A child prodigy, Millais grew up to be a hugely successful artist. Queen Victoria admired his work, and by the time he died, he was one of the wealthiest men in Victorian England.

June 8, 1829
Millais is born.

1840
Enters the Royal Academy.

1848
Founds the Pre-Raphaelite Brotherhood with the painters Holman Hunt and Dante Gabriel Rossetti.

1852
Exhibits *Ophelia*.

1855
Marries Effie Ruskin.

1886
Paints *Bubbles* which is later used on a poster for Pears soap.

1896
Elected president of the Royal Academy.

August 13, 1896
Dies in London.

Millais painted this self portrait when he was 18.

When he was just 11 years old, John Everett Millais became the youngest-ever student at the most prestigious art school in London, the Royal Academy, but he was soon frustrated by the Academy's old-fashioned rules.

When he was 19, he and some other artists founded a secret society, the 'Pre-Raphaelite Brotherhood', to create a radical new form of art. The artists of the 'PRB' were inspired by nature, and by artistic styles from the time before the Italian painter Raphael. Soon art critics knew all about the Brotherhood, and they weren't impressed.

A profitable friendship

Millais's fortunes changed when he and his friends were publicly supported by the most famous art critic in England, John Ruskin. Millais and Ruskin soon became good friends, even going on vacation together. But one summer in Scotland, Millais fell in love with Ruskin's wife, Effie. Ruskin and Effie were unhappily married, and within two years, Effie had left her husband and married Millais. Surprisingly, Ruskin and Millais remained good friends.

OPHELIA

Millais was just 22 years old when he began work on *Ophelia*, based on a scene from Shakespeare's play, *Hamlet*. The model for Ophelia was a 19-year-old girl named Elizabeth Siddal.

Millais lived and worked in a grand house in Kensington, London.

Fame and fortune

The Pre-Raphaelite Brotherhood fell apart after a few years, but Millais went from success to success. He made increasingly patriotic or sentimental pictures that he knew people would love. By the time he died, he was President of the Royal Academy, and a favorite painter of Queen Victoria.

Edouard Manet

1832 - 1883

This portait of Manet was made by his friend Henri Fantin-Latour in 1867. Manet was known for being impeccably well-dressed, polite and charming.

Edouard Manet wanted to be a respected artist, but his paintings caused scandal after scandal. By the time he received the recognition he craved, it was too late.

Manet grew up in a wealthy household in Paris, the son of an adoring mother and a strict father. As a child, all he wanted to do was paint. But his father had other ideas. He wanted him to join the navy, and it was only after Edouard failed his naval exams – twice – that he was finally allowed to study art, at a studio in Paris.

An accidental rebel

As a young painter, Manet was desperate to be accepted by the Salon, the official art exhibition in Paris, but his works kept being rejected. When his painting *The Luncheon on the Grass* was shown at another exhibition – the 'Salon of Refused Artists' – it outraged Parisian society, as it showed a naked woman sitting in a public park. Two years later, Manet painted another female nude, *Olympia*, which caused even more uproar. Manet was so upset, he fled to Spain to recover.

Manet made this illustration of 'The Raven', a scary story by Edgar Allan Poe, in 1875.

January 23, 1832
Edouard Manet is born in Paris.

1850
He enters Thomas Couture's studio in Paris.

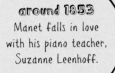

around 1853
Manet falls in love with his piano teacher, Suzanne Leenhoff.

1862
Suzanne Leenhoff has a son, Leon. Manet is probably his father, but he calls Leon his godson, to avoid a scandal.

1862
Manet's father dies. He becomes independently wealthy.

1863
He marries Suzanne Leenhoff, and exhibits *The Luncheon on the Grass*.

Manet's gang

Although the Salon was still rejecting his work, by the 1870s Manet was inspiring a new generation of artists: the Impressionists. Every Thursday, he met up with artists including Degas, Monet, and Renoir, to discuss artistic ideas. The group became known as 'Manet's gang'.

By the late 1870s, the critics were beginning to appreciate Manet's sketchy style and his vivid scenes of modern life. In 1881, he received one of the highest awards in France, the Légion d'Honneur, but Manet said success had come, 'twenty years too late.' By now, he was seriously ill, suffering from paralysis in his legs. On April 20, 1883, he had his left foot amputated. Ten days later, he died.

A BAR AT THE FOLIES-BERGÈRE
Manet used a real Folies barmaid, named Suzon, as the model for this painting, set in a famous Parisian nightclub.

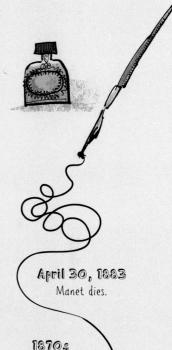

April 30, 1883
Manet dies.

1870s
Manet begins to suffer from syphilis and rheumatism.

1874
Manet paints with Monet in Argenteuil. His paintings become lighter and brighter.

1865
Olympia, Manet's painting of a naked woman looking directly at the viewer, causes a scandal.

1868
Manet meets Impressionist artist, Berthe Morisot. She persuades him to paint outdoors.

Edgar Degas

1834–1917

Edgar Degas painted many subjects, but is most famous as a painter of dancers. He made over 1,500 dance pictures, not only because he loved dancers, but because he said he wanted to 'capture movement itself'.

SELF PORTRAIT IN A BROWN VEST

Edgar Degas was born in Paris, the eldest son of a wealthy and well-connected family. He loved to paint and, by the age of 18, he had turned a room in the family home into his studio.

His father wanted him to study law, so Degas enrolled in law school. But he paid more attention to sketching in museums and, a couple of years later, he switched to studying art.

At first, he mainly painted serious pictures showing scenes from history. But, gradually, he turned to everyday subjects, such as horse racing, theaters and, most of all, ballet dancers, creating pastel drawings, prints and sculptures as well as paintings.

In this sketch, Degas captured the energy of a racehorse with just a few strokes.

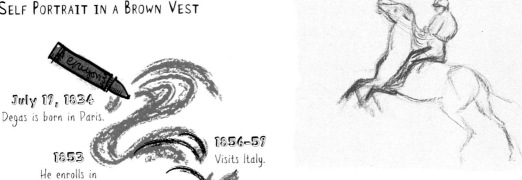

July 19, 1834
Degas is born in Paris.

1853
He enrolls in law school.

1855
Enrolls in art school.

1856–59
Visits Italy.

1865
He has his first picture accepted by an official exhibition.

1870–71
France at war with Prussia. Degas joins the National Guard.

DANCERS IN THE CLASSROOM

Degas loved to create unusual, behind-the-scenes views, like this painting of a ballet class. He was as likely to show a dancer adjusting her costume or relaxing during a break as performing an actual dance.

Earning a living

Degas's career was interrupted when war broke out in 1870. He joined the French National Guard and no longer had time for art. After the war, his father died and family debts forced Degas to sell his home and his art collection. For the first time in his life, he had to make a living from art. In search of buyers, he helped to organize a series of exhibitions with other artists, including Monet. Slowly, Degas began to make money.

In old age, Degas shut himself away in his studio, determined to devote himself to art, although he became increasingly lonely. He also suffered from terrible eye problems, but stubbornly kept sketching and sculpting from memory, almost until his death.

LITTLE DANCER AGED **14**

Degas caused a sensation with this lifelike sculpture.

1872–73
He visits his brother in New Orleans, U.S.A.

1874
First 'Impressionist' exhibition with Monet.

1880s
Degas takes up photography.

September 27, 1917
Degas dies.

Claude Monet

1840-1926

SELF PORTRAIT WITH A BERET

As a young artist, Claude Monet struggled to make a living. But he went on to become one of the world's most popular artists, famous for his bright, sketchy paintings in a style that became known as 'Impressionist'.

Claude Monet grew up in the French port of Le Havre. He hated school but had a talent for drawing. His father, a grocer, hoped his son would follow him into the trade. But instead, with the help of his aunt and a local landscape painter, he went on to study art in Paris.

Monet didn't do much better at art school, which he found stuffy and old-fashioned. But he did meet other young artists there, including Pierre-Auguste Renoir, who shared his passion for painting outdoors. Together, they began going on trips to the countryside, to study the changing effects of sunlight and weather.

November 14, 1840
Monet is born in Paris.

1845
Monet's parents move to Le Havre.

> School always gave me the impression I was in prison.

1857
Monet leaves school.

1859
He goes to Paris to study art.

Some of Monet's earliest works, like this sketch of an actor named Félix, were caricatures of people he'd seen.

1867
His son Jean is born.

1868
Tries to drown himself.

1870
Monet and Camille marry.

1870-71
War between France and Prussia (now part of Germany); Monet flees to England.

1871
Returns to France.

1874
Monet and his friends hold their first 'Impressionist' exhibition.

1878
Birth of second son, Michel.

Struggling along

Painting outdoors was hard work. Weighed down with sketchbooks, easel, canvases, brushes and boxes of paints, Monet braved wind, rain and even snow, wrapped in blankets and clutching a hot-water bottle to try to keep himself warm.

But, despite his efforts, Monet sold very few pictures. To people at the time, used to more somber, polished paintings, his sunny colors and sketchy brushwork were just too new and shocking. Sometimes he was so short of money, he only had beans to eat, and things got harder after the birth of his son, Jean.

This is Monet's actual mixing palette, showing the bright colors he liked to use.

WOMAN WITH A PARASOL
Camille dressed up and posed for many of Monet's pictures including this breezy outdoor scene, which also includes their son, Jean.

Struggling to support his young family, Monet even thought about drowning himself in a river.

But with help from friends and a few picture sales, he finally scraped together enough to rent a little house in the country. Now, he and his wife, Camille, could settle down — at least until war broke out in France. To escape the fighting, they fled across the sea to England.

1879
Camille dies.

1883
Moves to Giverny in northern France.

1890
Buys the Giverny house and begins work on the garden.

1891
Ernest Hoschedé dies.

1892
Monet marries Alice.

1907
Starts to suffer eye problems.

1911
Alice dies.

5th December, 1926
Monet dies and is buried at Giverny.

Putting on a show

After the war, Monet returned to Paris, but he struggled to get his pictures into official exhibitions, so he and his friends decided to hold their own exhibitions. Some critics mocked Monet's paintings, calling them 'palette-scrapings', but others praised him and, slowly, he began to find buyers. One, Ernest Hoschedé, invited Monet to his home – and he stayed for months.

This photograph shows Monet in front of the house at Giverny, where he lived after Camille's death. The house was surrounded by a huge garden.

They became so close that a year later, when Ernest ran out of money, Monet invited Ernest, his wife Alice and their children to live with him.

But things weren't all happy. Camille's health was failing and she died soon after the birth of their second son. Grief-stricken, Monet threw himself into painting while Alice looked after the children. A few years later, they moved to a new home in the village of Giverny.

Making it big

At last, Monet was making it. Sales were on the up, a show in New York was a huge hit and reviews called him 'a poet of nature'. Always a lover of fine clothes, food and flowers – often splashing out on luxuries even when he was broke – Monet could finally afford to pay for them. He also began to create his dream garden.

As he grew older, Monet had to wear tinted glasses and have an operation on his eyes.

My garden is my most beautiful masterpiece.

WATER LILIES AT GIVERNY
The flowers in this painting are made up of swirling streaks and splotches of color, while patches of green and blue suggest reflections of trees and sky.

Monet's garden

At Giverny, Monet dammed a river to create an enormous pond, which he filled with hundreds of water lilies, despite the protests of local farmers who feared his exotic plants would poison the water. Monet made painting after painting of his pond, working from dawn until dusk, often on huge, wall-sized canvases.

By now, Monet was suffering from serious eye problems, but he kept working. By the time of his death, aged 86, he had completed around 250 lily paintings, which now hang in museums and galleries around the world.

Some of Monet's lily pictures were so big, he had to have this enormous studio built in his garden to work on them.

Pierre-Auguste Renoir

1841–1919

Renoir in 1885

Pierre-Auguste Renoir found fame and fortune painting pictures that sparkle with light and color – especially pretty portraits of women and children.

Renoir made delicate drawings in chalk, like these sketches of a little child.

The son of a tailor, Renoir's earliest drawings were made on the floor with pieces of tailor's chalk. After he left school, he worked in a factory, painting flowers onto china cups. But when new machines put him out of a job, he decided to become an artist.

Renoir went to Paris to study. There he met other artists, including Monet, who became a lifelong friend. They were both struggling to earn a living, and shared a studio to save money. Then, war broke out and Renoir spent the next year in the cavalry, even though he knew nothing about horses.

Paris life

After the war, Renoir returned to art and put on an exhibition with Monet, and others, hoping to find more buyers. As the years passed, he scraped a living painting portraits. But, in his spare time, he would head to Paris's poorest districts, to paint sketchy, colorful scenes of the locals enjoying themselves.

Why shouldn't art be pretty? There are enough unpleasant things in the world.

February 25, 1841
Renoir is born in Limoges, France.

1844
The Renoir family moves to Paris.

1854
Renoir leaves school and gets a job in a china factory.

1861
Enrolls in art school.

1870–71
War between France and Prussia.

1874
First 'Impressionist' exhibition with Monet.

Love and success

One of Renoir's models, a lively redhead named Aline, became his girlfriend and, later, his wife. She appears in some of his best-known pictures, including *The Luncheon of the Boating Party*, below.

As Renoir sold more pictures, he and Aline could afford to travel. A trip to see art in Italy led him to try a new, smoother style. Then, after the birth of their sons, the couple moved to the country, where Renoir focused on painting beautiful women and family scenes.

THE LUNCHEON OF THE BOATING PARTY
This is one of Renoir's most ambitious pictures. It took him six months to finish, using friends and colleagues as his models. You can see Aline on the left, holding a small dog.

This photograph shows Renoir working in his studio in later life, when he was confined to a wheelchair.

In old age, Renoir suffered from arthritis. Hoping a warm climate would help, he and his family moved to southern France. The arthritis hurt his hands, but he bandaged them and worked on. By now he was rich and famous, but he remained modest. Just before he died, he said of his art: 'I think I'm beginning to understand something about it.'

December 3, 1919
Renoir dies.

1902
Arthritis makes it increasingly difficult for him to point.

1880
Meets Aline.

1885
Renoir's first son, Pierre, is born, followed by Jean in 1894 and Claude in 1901.

1890
He marries Aline.

Paul Cézanne

1839–1906

This photograph shows Cézanne in his best clothes. He usually worked in a smock.

Cézanne's rough, experimental way of painting – and rougher manners – often made him unpopular. But his unique approach filled many artists with admiration and had an influence on the development of modern art.

Cézanne was born into a wealthy family in southern France. His father, a banker, didn't want him to be an artist, so, to begin with, he studied law. But in the end, he rebelled and took up art.

As an art student in Paris, Cézanne developed a deliberately crude, bold style, slapping and smearing paint onto his canvas with a palette knife. Fellow students laughed at the result, but a few older artists admired it – though Cézanne distrusted their compliments. He was painfully awkward and made few friends, though he did begin a relationship with a bookseller named Hortense.

January 17, 1839
Cézanne is born in Aix-en-Provence, in southern France.

1857
Takes drawing classes at local art school.

1859
Enrolls in law school.

1861
Goes to Paris to study art.

1869
Meets Hortense and begins secret relationship.

1872
Birth of son Paul.

1886
Marries Hortense.

1875
Has first one-man show.

October 23, 1906
Cézanne dies of pneumonia after painting outside in a thunderstorm.

1907
A memorial exhibition seals his reputation as one of the most important modern artists.

STILL LIFE WITH ORANGES AND APPLES

I will astonish Paris with an apple.

Paris to Provence

Cézanne worked hard, but his pictures were turned down by official art shows, and critics called him a madman. In fits of despair, he would break his brushes and throw his pictures away. It was a difficult time, and he had to rely on his father for money.

A few years later, he returned home and began painting the local scenery in his distinctive style. He became so reclusive that some of his acquaintances thought he had died. Finally, as people's ideas about art changed, a curious art dealer tracked him down and organized a one-man show that won him huge acclaim.

A view of the mountain of Sainte-Victoire today

THE MOUNTAIN OF SAINTE-VICTOIRE

Cézanne painted this mountain again and again, from lots of viewpoints. His way of building up scenes using solid shapes and shifting views had a great influence on later artists, including Picasso.

Cézanne was so shy, he would run away if he saw a stranger while out sketching.

In old age, Cézanne stubbornly kept going on painting trips. One day he was caught in a thunderstorm and collapsed on the way back. A passing farmer carried him home, where he died days later.

Paul Gauguin

EUGÈNE HENRI PAUL GAUGUIN
1848–1903

This photograph of Gauguin playing a harmonium was taken in 1895, in the Paris studio of another artist, Alfonse Mucha.

Born with a restless spirit, Gauguin left his family and a career in stockbroking to become an artist. He spent the rest of his life in pursuit of paradise, painting many rich, exotic pictures of life in the South Pacific.

Paul Gauguin was born in Paris. He was part French, part Peruvian and spent his early childhood in Peru. The family returned to France when he was 7, but as soon as he was old enough, he went to sea.

At 23, Gauguin got a job with a Paris stockbroker, and seemed ready to settle down. By his early 30s, he was married with five children and a house in the suburbs. But he dreamed of becoming a painter. In 1882, the stockmarket crashed, and Gauguin seized the opportunity to leave his job and follow his dream.

BRETON GIRLS DANCING, PONT-AVEN

Gauguin developed his style in Pont-Aven in Brittany, where he was inspired by the landscape and the folk traditions of the Breton people. He said, 'I love Brittany. I find the wild and the primitive here.'

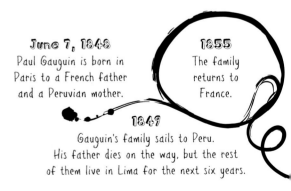

June 7, 1848
Paul Gauguin is born in Paris to a French father and a Peruvian mother.

1849
Gauguin's family sails to Peru. His father dies on the way, but the rest of them live in Lima for the next six years.

1855
The family returns to France.

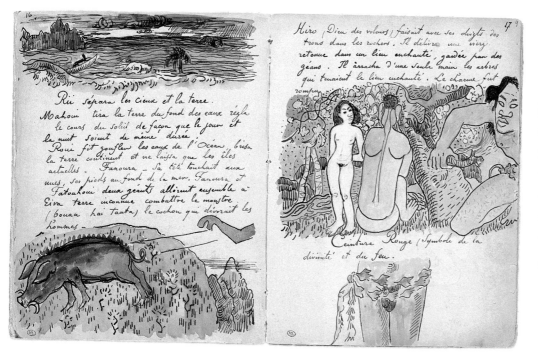

Everywhere he went, Gauguin kept detailed sketchbooks, such as this one from Tahiti. He often used the drawings and notes he made as the starting points for his paintings.

Seeking simplicity

Before long, Gauguin had spent his savings without selling any paintings. Unable to support his family, he left them, to go to Pont-Aven in Brittany, then to Panama and Martinique. He hoped to find a simpler way of life in the tropics, but poverty and a fever soon forced him to return to France.

Over the next couple of years, Gauguin won the admiration of other artists in France, but his paintings still weren't selling. With hopes of finding a tropical paradise, he set sail for Tahiti in the South Pacific in 1891.

In Tahiti, he immersed himself as much as possible in local culture and traditions. And it was there that he would produce many of his most famous paintings.

This is Gauguin's house on Tahiti where he produced bold, bright paintings of tropical island life.

1865–71
Serves three years on a merchant ship, then three years in the French navy.

1871
Gauguin begins work at a Paris stockbrokers.

1873
Marries Mette Gad – they go on to have five children.

1883
Quits his job to become a professional painter.

1884
Moves to Copenhagen, but returns to Paris the following year.

1886
Stays at Pont-Aven.

Gauguin used bright colors and bold shapes in this painting to show the stages of life from the baby on the right, to the old woman on the left.

The House of Pleasure

However, life in Tahiti wasn't as simple or as easy as Gauguin had hoped. He said he wanted to 'live like a native' there, but he didn't know how to hunt or fish, so he ended up living off expensive canned food imported from Europe. After two years, he had run out of money, and went back to Paris laden with paintings to sell.

Gauguin was in despair when he painted this, in 1897. He was ill, in debt and, despite having left his family years before, he was devastated to find out that his daughter had died. He even tried to poison himself.

In 1895, Gauguin returned to Tahiti. It was a creative time for him, but he struggled with ill health and growing debt. After falling out with local officials, he left Tahiti to settle in the Marquesas Islands. There, he built his last home, which he called 'the House of Pleasure'. At last, his work was selling in Paris, but he wasn't able to enjoy the success. His health deteriorated, and in 1903, he died.

1887
Works in Panama building the canal; travels to Martinique.

1891
Moves to Tahiti.

1893
Returns to Paris.

May 8, 1903
Dies in the Marquesas, age 54.

1888
Returns to Pont-Aven; stays with van Gogh in Arles.

1901
Moves to the Marquesas Islands.

1895
Goes back to Tahiti.

Gauguin's grave in the Marquesas

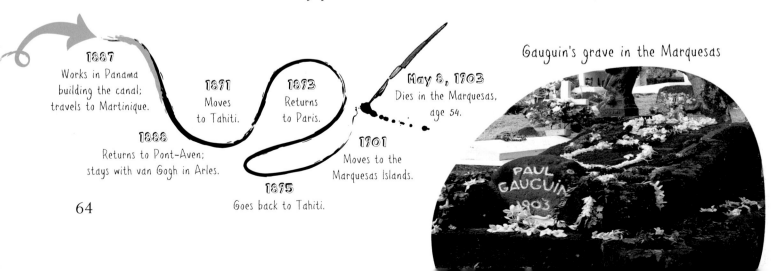

PAUL GAUGUIN 1903

Vincent van Gogh

1853–1890

Today van Gogh's paintings hang in galleries all around the world, and sell for tens of millions. But during his lifetime, he sold only one. His career as an artist lasted just ten years, but he painted compulsively, producing nearly 900 paintings. Tragically, he suffered periods of mental illness and committed suicide when he was 37.

SELF PORTRAIT AS AN ARTIST
This is one of 35 self portraits van Gogh painted.

Vincent was especially close to his brother Theo. When they were apart, he regularly sent him letters and sketches telling him about his work.

Vincent van Gogh was one of six children of a Dutch preacher. As a young man, he worked as an art dealer, a teacher, a bookseller and a preacher.

It wasn't until he was 27 that van Gogh decided to become an artist. His first paintings were muddy-toned scenes of poor workers. He hoped they would make his name as an artist, but no one bought them.

Out of money, and needing a change, he went to stay with his brother Theo in Paris. He studied painting there, and met other artists, including Paul Gauguin. Influenced by them, he began using much brighter colors.

In search of sun

Van Gogh found city life stressful. He drank heavily, and had a quick temper that landed him in arguments. After two years, he left Paris, and settled in Arles, in southern France, where he enjoyed the sunshine and color. He rented rooms in a little yellow house, and invited Gauguin to stay. He made a series of cheerful paintings, including several pictures of sunflowers, to welcome him.

This is a detail from a sketch van Gogh made of his house in Arles.

Van Gogh was very messy. Sometimes, he even cleaned his brushes on his socks.

THE BEDROOM AT ARLES
This is one of a series of bright paintings van Gogh made to decorate the house.

He wanted to express 'absolute restfulness' with this painting.

Gauguin spent two months in Arles. But the two men argued fiercely. When van Gogh threatened him with a razor, Gauguin fled. Suffering from mental illness, van Gogh turned on himself. He cut off part of his ear and gave it to a local girl, before being taken to hospital.

Van Gogh's illness grew worse. Eventually he admitted himself to a mental hospital in St. Rémy. There, he continued to paint feverishly, finishing about a picture a day – dramatic scenes, filled with intense colors and wild, swirling lines.

1853
Vincent van Gogh is born in Groot Zundert, the Netherlands.

1869–1876
Works as an art dealer in London, Paris and The Hague.

1878
Works as a teacher in London.

1878–1879
Works as a lay preacher in Belgium.

1880
Decides to become an artist.

1885
Has his first exhibition in a paint shop window in Antwerp.

1886–88
Lives in Paris; meets Paul Gauguin.

WHEATFIELD WITH CROWS

Van Gogh made this painting in the last weeks of his life. Some people have suggested that the gloomy sky reflects his troubled state of mind, but his use of paint shows great control.

Final years

After a year, van Gogh seemed to be getting better. He moved north, to Auvers-sur-Oise, to be near Theo. Under the care of Dr. Paul Gachet, he tried to put his illness out of his mind and concentrate on painting.

But he became desperately worried about being a burden to his brother, and felt he had failed as an artist. Overcome by depression, he shot himself in the chest. He died two days later, at the age of 37, with Theo at his bedside. At his funeral, his coffin was covered in sunflowers.

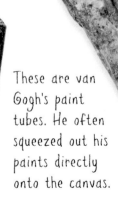

These are van Gogh's paint tubes. He often squeezed out his paints directly onto the canvas.

February 1888
Moves to Arles.

May 1889
Admits himself to a mental hospital in St. Rémy.

1889
His work is exhibited in Paris.

1890
The Red Vineyard is sold. It's the only painting van Gogh sells in his lifetime.

May 1890
Moves to Auvers-sur-Oise, near Paris.

July 27, 1890
Van Gogh dies after shooting himself.

Gustav Klimt

1862-1918

This photograph shows Klimt with his pet cat.

Gustav Klimt is famous for creating rich, decorative paintings that shimmer with gold leaf and bright, jewel-like colors. But, although he won some prestigious prizes, his bold use of nude figures in his drawings and paintings shocked many viewers in his day.

Klimt was born in Vienna, the second of seven children. His father was a gold engraver, who struggled to support his large family.

Klimt left school at 14, to study decorative painting at art school. He went on to set up a company with one of his brothers to create wall paintings. The company was doing well when they were hired to decorate a ceiling for the local university. Klimt's designs – which included many nude figures – caused an uproar. Some viewers called them 'perverted'.

Klimt refused to accept any more public jobs. He also left the official artists' association of Vienna and set up a breakaway group of artists, known as the Secession. The group had its own magazine and art shows, and dreamed of transforming society through art.

Klimt designed this poster for one of the Secession's art shows.

July 14, 1862
Klimt is born in Vienna, Austria.

1876-83
He studies at art school.

1880s-90s
He forms a company working on wall paintings.

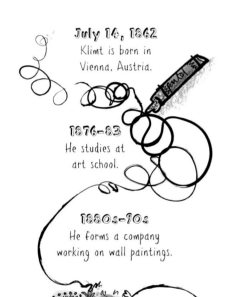

1890s
Begins to holiday on Lake Attersee.

1894
Asked to design ceiling paintings for a university hall.

1897
Forms a breakaway artists' group known as the Secession.

1903
Visits the famous golden mosaics in Ravenna, Italy.

1905
Leaves the Secession.

1908
His most famous painting, *The Kiss*, is bought by the Austrian government.

February 6, 1918
Klimt dies, age 56.

Golden age

During vacation on Lake Attersee, near Vienna, Klimt had begun to paint detailed, jewel-bright landscapes. He was also becoming a sought-after portrait artist, creating pictures of fashionable women in elaborately patterned dresses, sometimes of his own design.

After a trip to see ancient golden mosaics in Italy, and influenced by his father, Klimt began adding gold leaf to his pictures. Probably the most famous example is *The Kiss*.

> Whoever wants to know something about me... ought to look carefully at my pictures.

In this photograph, you can see Klimt and a friend, fashion designer Emilie Flöge, on vacation at Lake Attersee. Some people think the couple in *The Kiss* was based on them.

THE KISS

Klimt covered large parts of this picture in real gold and silver leaf, to create a rich, glittering surface.

As Klimt grew older, he began working on large scenes of figures symbolizing life and death. Then, he suffered a stroke, followed by pneumonia, and died shortly afterwards.

Henri Matisse

1869 - 1954

This photo shows Matisse in his studio in 1913.

This is Collioure, in the south of France, where Matisse spent the summer in 1905. Having grown up in the north, the bright sunshine and vibrant colors of the south were a revelation to him.

Matisse initially trained as a lawyer, but he went on to become one of the most influential artists of the 20th century. He used bright, bold colors and believed art should give comfort, 'like a good armchair'.

Henri Matisse's parents, a shopkeeper and a hat maker, had high hopes for him and sent him to Paris to train as a lawyer. But when he was 20, he had appendicitis, and while recovering in bed, he took up painting. It was then that he decided to become an artist.

Matisse returned to Paris – this time, to study art. At first, he struggled for money, but in 1898 he married Amélie Parayre and she set herself up as a hat maker to support him. She posed as a model for many of his paintings, as well as having two sons with him and taking care of his daughter from a previous relationship.

THE ROOFS OF COLLIOURE
Matisse made this painting while spending the summer with fellow artist André Derain, and experimenting with a new, colorful style.

Wild art

In 1905, Matisse exhibited his paintings in Paris. Many critics disliked his style, which used bright, unnatural colors, rather than showing things as they really looked. One called him a 'fauve' (French for wild beast) and the name stuck.

Despite the controversy, Matisse's work began to sell. The family moved into a large house in a suburb of Paris, and he visited North Africa and the Mediterranean for inspiration.

In 1917, angry critics burned a copy of one of Matisse's paintings outside the Chicago gallery where it was on show.

HARMONY IN RED

Like many of Matisse's paintings, this shows his love of richly patterned fabrics. His hometown was noted for its weavers, and he grew up admiring the sumptuous, bright silks produced there.

As well as his paintings and drawings, Matisse produced several sculptures, mostly of human figures.

When I started to paint, I felt transported into a kind of paradise.

Matisse used charcoal fixed to a long pole to draw the outlines for his large wall paintings.

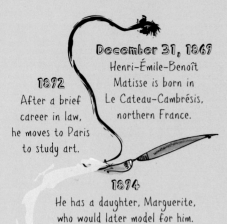

December 31, 1869
Henri-Émile-Benoît Matisse is born in Le Cateau-Cambrésis, northern France.

1892
After a brief career in law, he moves to Paris to study art.

1894
He has a daughter, Marguerite, who would later model for him.

Harmony in color

After spending more and more time in the south of France, Matisse finally settled in Nice in 1917. There, he lived through difficult times. In 1939, he separated from his wife and the Second World War broke out. Two years later, he had two major operations that left him mostly confined to a wheelchair or to his bed. Still, he found peace and harmony in his work, painting calm interiors, sunny views through windows, goldfish and voluptuous women.

1898
Marries Amélie Parayre. They later have two sons.

1905
Exhibits his work in Paris and is labeled a 'fauve'. Meets and befriends Pablo Picasso.

1917
Moves to Nice.

1929-30
Travels to America and Tahiti; begins two murals for an American art collector.

1939
Matisse separates from Amélie.

WOMAN WITH A PURPLE COAT
The model for this, and many other paintings, was Matisse's assistant, Lydia Delektorskaya.

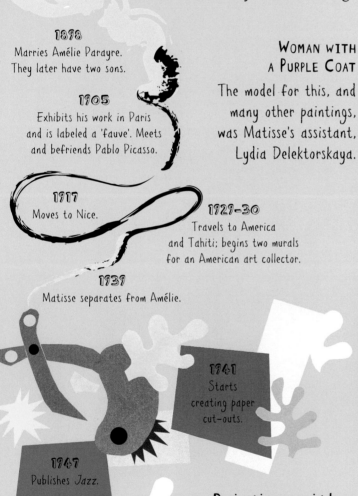

1941
Starts creating paper cut-outs.

1947
Publishes *Jazz*.

1948-51
Works on the Chapel of the Rosary in Vence.

November 3, 1954
Dies in Nice, age 84.

Painting with scissors

By his mid-70s, Matisse was too ill to paint. But this didn't stop his creativity. He developed a new technique which he called 'painting with scissors'. This involved cutting painted paper into shapes and making lively compositions with them.

un moment de libres.
Ne devrait-on
pas faire ac-
complir un
grand voyage
en avion aux
jeunes gens
ayant terminé
leurs études.
54

ICARUS

This is one of 20 color plates based on paper cut-outs that Matisse made for his book, *Jazz*.

Matisse, in his bed, working on paper cut-outs in 1949.

Final fate

Matisse's last major project was to create wall paintings and stained glass windows, based on his paper cut-outs, for a hillside chapel in the town of Vence where he lived, near Nice. He was persuaded to take on the job by a nun who had been a model for him in her youth.

Matisse saw it as the culmination of his career, but was too weak to attend the opening ceremony in 1951. Three years later, he died of a heart attack.

Wassily Kandinsky

1866–1944

Here you can see Kandinsky working on one of his paintings.

Kandinsky helped to invent the idea of 'abstract' art: making shapes and colors into pictures, instead of painting real-life scenes. He said he had gotten the idea when he accidentally looked at a painting upside down, and was moved to tears by its beauty.

Wassily Kandinsky nearly wasn't an artist at all. He was born in Russia and, after a musical upbringing, he decided to study law and economics. He only took up art seriously at the age of 30.

He moved to Germany to study, and quickly made his mark as both an artist and a writer. He began to explore the possibilities of abstract painting, and helped to found an influential journal called *The Blue Rider*. In his writings, he said art should be about spiritual ideas, and often likened it to music.

This is Kandinsky's painting palette. It shows the vivid, pure colors he liked to use.

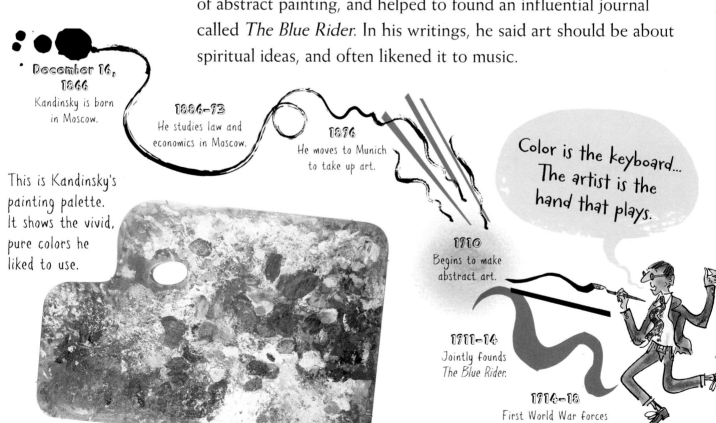

December 16, 1866
Kandinsky is born in Moscow.

1886–93
He studies law and economics in Moscow.

1896
He moves to Munich to take up art.

1910
Begins to make abstract art.

1911–14
Jointly founds *The Blue Rider*.

1914–18
First World War forces Kandinsky to return to Russia.

Color is the keyboard... The artist is the hand that plays.

Troubled times

The years leading up to the First World War were tense. As war drew closer, Kandinsky began a series of paintings based on ideas of death and rebirth, including *Composition No. 6*.

At the outbreak of war, Kandinsky went home to Russia. When it was over, he moved back to Germany to teach at an influential school of art and architecture, known as the Bauhaus. Here, he developed a more geometric, clean-edged style.

But the Nazis were rising to power. They closed the Bauhaus, condemned Kandinsky and other modern artists as 'degenerate' and burned their work. Kandinsky fled to France. A few years later, the Second World War began. Kandinsky would not live to see it end. He died in France, aged 77.

This photograph shows Kandinsky's storeroom, full of mural-painting materials, at the Bauhaus.

1922–33
Teaches at the Bauhaus, but leaves Germany after the school is closed by the Nazis.

1937
The Nazis burn three of Kandinsky's paintings.

1939
On the eve of the Second World War, Kandinsky becomes a French citizen.

December 13, 1944
Kandinsky dies in France.

Pablo Picasso

1881–1973

Picasso signed this early photograph for some friends.

A child prodigy, Pablo Picasso went on to become probably the most famous artist of modern times. He was amazingly versatile, working in a huge range of styles and materials – from delicate pastels to bold geometric paintings, ground-breaking collages, ceramics, sculptures and theater designs.

Pablo Picasso grew up in southern Spain. His father was an art teacher and, according to his mother, baby Pablo began drawing before he could talk. At age 13, he won a place at art school. But he found the lessons disappointing and eventually dropped out.

After he left school, Picasso moved to Paris, which was the capital of the art world at that time. There, he began painting moody, blue-toned scenes of beggars and outcasts, in what became known as his 'Blue Period'. He had almost no money and had to share a cramped apartment, taking turns sleeping in the only bed. Sometimes, he even burned his pictures just to keep warm.

October 25, 1881
Pablo Ruiz Picasso is born in Malaga, southern Spain.

1890
He starts painting.

1894
He studies art in Barcelona.

1900
He moves to Paris.

This photograph from around 1900 shows the area of Paris where Picasso lived.

1906
Begins to develop Cubism with Braque.

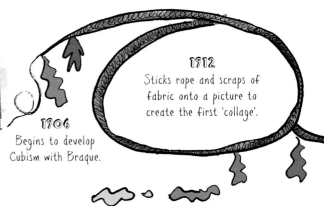

1912
Sticks rope and scraps of fabric onto a picture to create the first 'collage'.

From blue to rose

Gradually, Picasso's blue pictures gave way to scenes of acrobats and circus folk tinged with orange and pink – his 'Rose Period'. And then came a daring experiment that would change the course of modern art...

Working closely with a friend, Georges Braque, Picasso began making pictures that broke things down into shapes and showed them from different viewpoints. The result was a strange, disjointed style known as Cubism, and it was to have a huge influence on other artists.

This painting from Picasso's Rose Period shows two circus performers in traditional costumes.

ACROBAT AND YOUNG HARLEQUIN, 1905

Love and marriage

As Picasso's reputation grew, he was asked to design a set and costumes for an experimental ballet. At work on this, he met a dark-haired dancer named Olga and fell in love. The two married the following year. Inspired by Olga, Picasso changed style again, creating huge, dreamy paintings of strong, serene women.

MOTHER AND CHILD, 1922
This drawing shows Olga and Paulo, Picasso's wife and son.

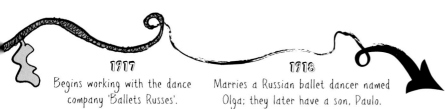

1917
Begins working with the dance company 'Ballets Russes'.

1918
Marries a Russian ballet dancer named Olga; they later have a son, Paulo.

This photograph, taken by Dora Maar, shows Picasso working on *Guernica*.

Fame and war

Picasso's art was a success, but his marriage wasn't. Eventually, he and Olga separated and Picasso began looking for inspiration in a string of other women – a young woman named Marie-Thérèse, a photographer named Dora Maar and a painter, Françoise Gilot.

Then civil war broke out in Spain. One particularly brutal incident, the bombing of civilians in a town called Guernica, caused outrage around the world and led Picasso to create one of his most famous paintings.

GUERNICA, 1937

Picasso took only three weeks to create this bleak Cubist picture of the terrible bombing at Guernica. The picture was exhibited in Paris and then around the world, to raise awareness of the atrocity.

1927
Picasso and Olga separate; Picasso meets Marie-Thérèse; they later have a daughter, Maya.

1936
Picasso meets Dora Maar.

1937
He creates *Guernica*.

1939–45
Second World War; Picasso remains in Paris.

1943
He meets Françoise; they later have two children, Claude and Paloma.

78

Success

A few years later, the Second World War engulfed Europe. Picasso stayed stubbornly in Paris while the city was occupied by German forces. The French Resistance helped to smuggle him art supplies.

After the war, Picasso's fame grew and grew. He tried to escape the spotlight by moving to the south of France, but he still had many visitors. As he grew older, he began to create pictures inspired by earlier artists. He also experimented with pottery, meeting a pottery worker named Jacqueline. She was his final inspiration.

In 1962, Picasso decorated this plate with a portrait of Jacqueline Picasso.

> Every child is an artist. The problem is how to remain an artist once you grow up.

Even in old age, Picasso kept working, creating a stream of colorful, expressive paintings and prints. He died in 1973, leaving a staggering number of works of art – probably around 50,000 – worth hundreds of millions.

Today, he is still one of world's most sought-after artists, and even the most stolen, with several museums dedicated to his work.

Picasso had many glamorous visitors. In this photograph, he is showing French movie star, Brigitte Bardot, around his studio.

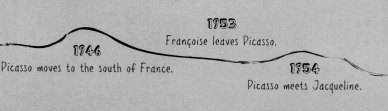

1946
Picasso moves to the south of France.

1953
Françoise leaves Picasso.

1954
Picasso meets Jacqueline.

1955
Olga dies.

1961
Picasso marries Jacqueline.

April 8, 1973
Picasso dies and is buried at his country home.

Edward Hopper

1882 – 1967

Hopper in his studio in Greenwich Village, New York.

Once, while he was at art school, he tricked a fellow student by painting bed bugs on paper, cutting them out and leaving them on his pillow.

AUTOMAT

Many of Hopper's paintings show people in public spaces, lost in private thought. Hopper used his wife Jo as the model for all the women in his paintings.

American artist Edward Hopper became famous for his paintings of modern life. He painted solitary people in big cities and eerie, abandoned buildings. His dramatically lit paintings have influenced many photographers and filmmakers.

Ever since he was a child growing up in New York, Edward Hopper had wanted to be an artist, but his parents had a more practical idea. They persuaded him to train as a commercial illustrator, which was a more reliable way of earning a living.

Illustration was a profession Hopper disliked intensely. In 1923, he became friends with a painter, Josephine Nivison. While he was reserved and secretive, she was outgoing and talkative. They fell in love, and were married a year later.

July 22, 1882
Edward Hopper is born.

80

Finding success

That same year, Hopper held an exhibition of his watercolors. It was such a success that he was able to give up his job and devote himself to painting.

For the rest of his life, Hopper followed a strict routine. He went to his studio every day and worked slowly, producing one or two paintings a year. He said that each painting was complete in his mind before he picked up a brush.

His reputation grew steadily, and by the time he died, his paintings were hanging in museums all over the United States.

Hopper's painting, *The House by the Railroad*, may have partly inspired the artist Charles Addams who created this *Addams Family* cartoon.

THE HOUSE BY THE RAILROAD

Hopper spotted this house from a train window.

May 15, 1967
Dies in his studio.
His wife Jo dies
a year later.

1960
Protests against abstract
art at the Whitney Museum
and the Museum of Modern
Art in New York.

1930
The House by the Railroad is
the first painting to enter the
collection of the Museum of
Modern Art in New York.

1900-1906
Studies at the New York School of Art.
Visits Paris, and is influenced
by the Impressionists.

1918
His poster *Smash the Hun*
wins first prize in a competition.

1924
Marries fellow artist
Josephine Verstille Nivison.

1924
Holds an exhibition of
watercolors, which sells
out. Is able to give up
commercial art.

René Magritte

1898-1967

Belgian artist René Magritte was a shy, ordinary-looking man, but his art was anything but ordinary. His paintings show strange, impossible events – such as a train steaming out of a fireplace, or businessmen floating in the sky. He wanted his paintings to make people think.

Magritte often dressed in a suit and bowler hat.

Magritte's childhood was full of unhappiness. His parents often moved from place to place, and when he was 14, his mother drowned herself. A year later, he began to study art. He held his first exhibition when he was 29 – but it received terrible reviews.

Magritte (right) with his wife, Georgette, and friends in Paris, dressed up in masks

Ceci n'est pas une pipe.

THIS IS NOT A PIPE

The writing in this painting reads, 'This is not a pipe' in French. Magritte wanted to point out that paintings were illusions. He liked saying, 'Of course it's not a pipe! Just try putting tobacco in it!'

Bitterly disappointed, Magritte left for Paris, where an exciting new group of artists was working. Known as the Surrealists, they weren't interested in recording ordinary reality. They thought that dreams could be more real than everyday life.

November 21, 1898
René Magritte is born.

1912
Magritte's mother drowns herself.

1922
Marries Georgette Berger, whom he had met when he was 15, at a town fair.

1927
Has his first solo exhibition, at the Galerie La Centaure, in Brussels.

1927-1930
Lives in Paris and becomes friends with Surrealist artists.

Back to Brussels

In Paris, Magritte worked at an incredible rate – in 1927 alone, he produced 60 paintings. But he found life in Paris exhausting, and in 1930, he returned to Brussels, where he lived and worked for the rest of his life.

Magritte was a very unusual artist. He never had a studio, and preferred to paint in his kitchen or his dining room at home. He didn't dress like an artist either: he wore a suit and a bowler hat, the clothes of a businessman. He rarely changed his painting style, and he worked steadily in Brussels until his death, in 1967.

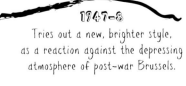

1947-8
Tries out a new, brighter style, as a reaction against the depressing atmosphere of post-war Brussels.

1948
To make money, he forges paintings and counterfeit bills.

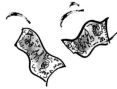

1965
Goes back to his old, pre-war style.

August 15, 1967
Magritte dies of cancer, age 68.

Salvador Dalí
1904-1989

Dalí in 1955, holding a magnifying glass

From an early age it was clear that Salvador Dalí had amazing artistic talent: he was only 15 years old when his paintings were first displayed in public. But his eccentric personality and bizarre performances became as famous as his sculptures and paintings.

This photograph shows Dalí painting at an easel. He used oil paints to produce very realistic textures and light effects.

Dalí's youth was marked by tragedy. He often visited the grave of a dead older brother and, when Dalí was 17, his mother died of cancer. When he went to art school in Madrid he didn't fit in, and he was eventually expelled for insulting his teachers. But he was still desperate to be an artist.

More than real

For the next few years, Dalí just drifted. But everything changed in 1929, when he went to Paris and met a group of young artists who called themselves the Surrealists. They felt frustrated with everyday life and tried to use their dreams and feelings to create art that was more than real, or 'surreal'. Dalí seized this idea eagerly. He started making dream-like paintings and films, and gave performances with strange costumes and unlikely props.

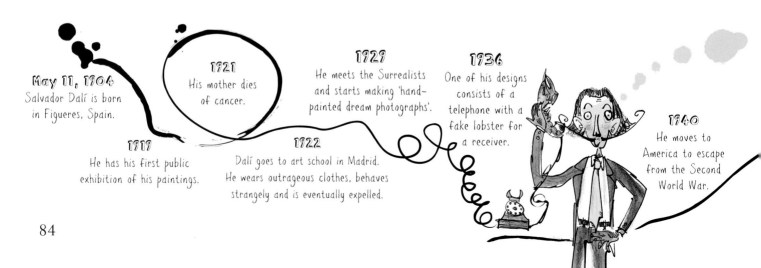

May 11, 1904
Salvador Dalí is born in Figueres, Spain.

1919
He has his first public exhibition of his paintings.

1921
His mother dies of cancer.

1922
Dalí goes to art school in Madrid. He wears outrageous clothes, behaves strangely and is eventually expelled.

1929
He meets the Surrealists and starts making 'hand-painted dream photographs'.

1936
One of his designs consists of a telephone with a fake lobster for a receiver.

1940
He moves to America to escape from the Second World War.

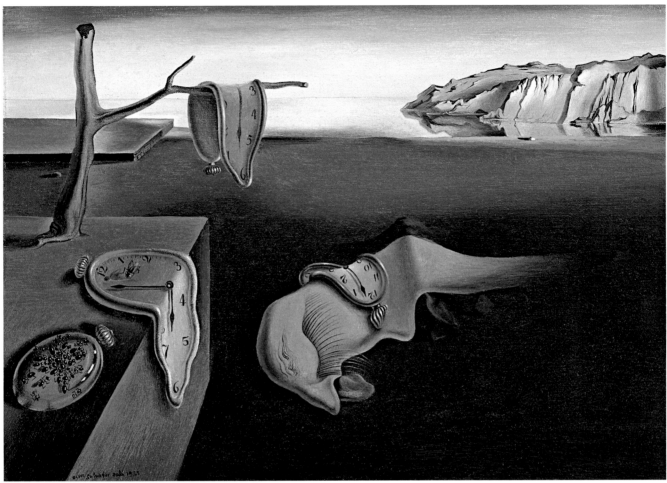

THE PERSISTENCE OF MEMORY

Dalí got the idea for the melting watches in this painting when he saw a round Camembert cheese melting in the sun. He called his paintings 'hand-painted dream photographs', meaning that they were accurate images of what he saw inside his head.

Really surreal

> The difference between the Surrealists and me is that I am a Surrealist.

Despite many arguments with the Surrealists, Dalí became by far the most famous Surrealist artist. In later life he remained as eccentric as ever, but he also branched out, advertising chocolates and creating a logo for a popular brand of lollipops. In 1960 he set up a museum and theater devoted to his work in his home town of Figueres, in Spain. He died there in 1989, at the age of 85.

1949
He moves back to Spain.

1960 onwards
He sets up the Dalí Museum and Theater in Figueres.

1984
He is badly burned during a fire at his house, and moves to live in his theater and museum.

January 23, 1989
Dalí dies.

85

Jackson Pollock
1912-1956

Pollock dripping paint onto a canvas on the floor

American artist Jackson Pollock soared to fame in the 1940s with an unusual way of making pictures. Instead of brushing paint onto his canvas, he dripped, poured and splashed it – earning him the nickname Jack the Dripper.

Jackson Pollock was born into a poor farming family in the western USA, the youngest of five brothers. One of his earliest experiences of art was of Native American sand paintings – made by trickling thin lines of colored sand onto the ground – which he saw on trips with his father.

A difficult person with a fierce temper, Pollock was expelled from school. He went on to study art in New York. There, at an experimental workshop, he first tried pouring and flinging paint. At the same time, he was battling depression. To try to tackle the problem, he started to see a therapist, who encouraged him to keep making art.

January 28, 1912
Jackson Pollock is born in Wyoming, and grows up in Arizona and California.

1928
He is expelled from high school.

1930
He moves to New York to study art.

1938
He is admitted to the hospital, suffering from depression.

1945
He marries Lee Krasner and moves to Long Island.

86

Escape to the country

Pollock rapidly became a successful artist. At one exhibition, he met an artist named Lee Krasner who greatly admired his work. A few years later, he and Lee married.

With help from a wealthy art dealer, the couple bought a house and barn in a peaceful part of Long Island, just outside New York City. Pollock turned the barn into a studio and set to work. Laying huge canvases flat on the floor, he splashed, squeezed and dripped paint on top, creating complex, swirling patterns full of energy and rhythm.

This is the floor of Pollock's studio. You can see how it became covered in paint.

BLUE POLES

This painting, filled with dancing loops and lines of color, helped to seal Pollock's reputation when a museum bought it for a record-breaking sum in the 1970s.

End of the road

By now, Pollock was producing many fine paintings. But he was still wrestling with depression and drinking too much. Eventually, things got so bad that he stopped painting. One night, while Lee was away, he went out driving, and was killed when his car overturned.

1947
Pollock develops his drip and splash technique.

1948
He holds a sell-out show in Manhattan.

1949
A magazine asks if he is the greatest living American artist.

August 11, 1956
Pollock dies in a car crash, age 44.

Andy Warhol

1928-1987

Warhol in his studio in 1965

Bold, brash and commercial, Warhol's art reflected his fascination with fame. His pictures of movie stars and advertising images captured, and helped to define, American popular culture in the 1960s and 70s.

Sam

Andrew Warhola was born in Pittsburgh, USA, to working-class immigrants from Eastern Europe. He studied pictorial design at college. Then, at 21, he packed his belongings in a paper grocery bag and moved to New York. Dropping the 'a' from the end of his last name, he made his name as an illustrator in the 1950s before finding fame as a painter in the 60s.

Having collected photographs of celebrities as a boy, Warhol now carefully created his own celebrity image. He wore a silver wig and sunglasses. This made him stand out, but also gave him a form of disguise to hide behind – he was actually rather shy.

SAM

This is one of a series of 25 cat portraits that Warhol produced as a book in 1954.

Warhol (far left) opened up his New York studio, the Factory, to a lively mix of poets, models, actors and other friends and followers.

August 6, 1928
Andy Warhol is born Andrew Warhola in Pittsburgh, Pennsylvania, USA.

1945
Studies painting and design. Works part-time as a shop window dresser.

1949
Moves to New York City where he works as a commercial illustrator.

ONE HUNDRED CAMPBELL'S SOUP CANS

This was one of the paintings Warhol exhibited in his first solo art show in 1962.

1960
Starts working as a painter.

1962
Has his first one-man art exhibition; founds his studio, the Factory; begins producing screenprints of celebrities and advertising images.

1963
Starts making movies.

In the future everyone will be world-famous for 15 minutes.

1965–67
Manages a rock band, The Velvet Underground, and designs their album cover with a banana on the front.

June 3, 1968
Valerie Solanas, a visitor to the Factory, shoots and nearly kills him.

1973
Admitted to hospital suffering pain from gallstones.

1985
Commissioned by Campbell's Soup Company to make a series of paintings of its soup products.

February 22, 1987
Dies, age 58, of a heart attack after a gall bladder operation. Buried wearing a silver wig and sunglasses.

Factory work

Although he produced paintings, photographs, sculptures and movies, some of Warhol's most famous works were screenprinted, which allowed him to make multiple copies at once. He even called his studio 'The Factory' to reflect the way he worked.

The Factory became a popular gathering place for artists and eccentrics, but in 1968, Warhol was shot by one of his visitors. After that, he made his studio more private and focused on painting portraits for celebrities. He died in 1987.

Glossary

People use a lot of specialist words to talk about art. This glossary explains some of the words you will find in this book – or you may come across elsewhere.

abstract art – art which does not show any recognizable people or scenes. Kandinsky pioneered this style.

action painting – an energetic way of painting by splashing and dripping paint, made famous by Jackson Pollock.

apprentice – a young person who learns a skill or trade from an experienced master.

art movement – a group of artists who work together and share ideas, and who often hold joint exhibitions.

camera obscura – meaning 'dark room' in Latin, it is a device for projecting images through a glass lens onto a flat surface.

caricature – a portrait that exaggerates part of a person's appearance or personality for comic effect.

canvas – cloth used for painting on, usually stretched over a wooden frame.

chiaroscuro – the use of strong contrasts of light and shade to produce drama in a picture.

collages – pictures made by gluing down bits of paper, cloth or other materials.

Cubism – a style developed by Picasso and Braque which shows the subject in a fragmented way, as if seen from different angles at the same time.

Fauves – from the French for 'wild beasts', this is the name given in 1905 to a group of painters, including Henri Matisse, who used vibrant, unnatural colors.

exhibition – a show of works of art.

fresco – a wall painting made by applying colors to wet plaster.

impasto – a very thick layer of paint. The word comes from the Italian for 'paste'.

Impressionism – an art movement founded in France in the 1870s by Claude Monet and his friends. They painted outdoors and developed a sketchy style, to try to capture the changing effects of natural light.

landscapes – pictures where a landscape or scenery is the main subject.

master painter – a painter in charge of a workshop, assistants and apprentices.

murals – wall paintings.

nudes – statues or pictures of naked figures.

oil paints – slow-drying paints made by mixing pigments and oil.

palette – a board on which an artist mixes paint colors. Also the name for the range of colors used by an artist.

pastels – soft, colored crayons.

patron – someone who buys art and supports artists.

pigment – a powdered substance used to give color to paints.

plaster – a smooth, quick-drying paste, often applied to walls before painting.

Pop art – an art movement that grew in the 1950s-60s which used images from popular culture, such as comic books and advertising. Andy Warhol was a famous Pop artist.

portraits – pictures of real people which try to capture their appearance or personality.

Pre-Raphaelite Brotherhood – a group of British artists, founded in 1848, who were inspired by art from the time before Raphael. They included John Everett Millais.

print – an image made by pressing an inked surface, such as a carved wood block or metal plate, onto paper. Often used to make many copies.

screenprinting – a method of printing where ink or paint is pressed through a stencil fixed to a silk panel onto paper or canvas.

sculpture – a statue or three-dimensional work of art.

sketch – a quick drawing or painting.

self portrait – a picture made by an artist of his or her own likeness.

still lifes – pictures mainly of objects that don't move, such as flowers, fruit and vases.

Surrealism – an art movement that started in 1920s Paris. Surrealists, such as Dalí and Magritte, used bizarre, dream-like images to explore unconscious ideas or feelings.

watercolors – paints made by mixing pigments and water.

About the pictures

The title for each work of art is given below, along with, wherever possible, the date it was made, the materials used, its dimensions (height x width) and where it can usually be seen. Where exact dates are not known, they are shown with a 'c.' in front of them.

cover pictures, Jan van Eyck (see note for page 8); Claude Monet (see note for page 54); Edouard Manet seated in his studio surrounded by other artists, print based on *Studio at Batignolles* by Henri Fantin-Latour, 1870, oil on canvas, Musée d'Orsay, Paris, France © Lebrecht Music and Arts Photo Library/Alamy; Rembrandt *Self Portrait as a Young Man*, c.1628, oil on panel, 22.5 x 19cm (9 x 7in) Rijksmuseum, Amsterdam © Bridgeman Art Library; Salvador Dalí © Sipa Press/Rex Features; Vincent van Gogh *Self Portrait*, 1889, oil on canvas, 65 x 54cm (25½ x 21in), Musée d'Orsay, Paris, France © The Gallery Collection/Corbis

page 2, close-up photo of Monet's paint palette (see note for page 55)

GIOTTO
page 6, Portrait of Giotto, detail from *Five Florentine Renaissance Masters* by Paolo Uccello, late 15th century, tempera on wood, 66 x 210cm (26 x 63in), Louvre, Paris, France © akg-images/Joseph Martin
page 7, photo of Arena Chapel (Cappella Scrovegni) in Padua, Italy © The Art Archive/Alamy
page 7, *Lamentation Over the Dead Christ*, c.1305, fresco, 200 x 185cm (79 x 73in), Arena Chapel, Padua, Italy © akg-images/Cameraphoto

JAN VAN EYCK
page 8, *Portrait of a Man* (probably a self portrait), 1433, oil on oak panel, 26 x 19cm (10 x 7½in), National Gallery, London, UK © The Art Gallery Collection/Alamy
page 8, photo of Bruges © Planet Seen/Alamy
page 9, *The Virgin and Child with Chancellor Rolin*, c.1435, oil on wood panel,

66 x 62cm (26 x 24in), Louvre, Paris, France © The Art Archive/Musée du Louvre Paris/Gianni Dagli Orti

LEONARDO DA VINCI
page 10, *Self Portrait as an Old Man*, c.1512, red chalk on paper, 33 x 21cm (13 x 8in), Biblioteca Reale, Turin, Italy © Bettmann/Corbis
page 10, pages from Leonardo's notebook, 1513-14, Bibliotheque de l'Institut de France, Paris, France © Giraudon/Bridgeman Art Library
pages 10-11 model of Leonardo da Vinci's flying machine, built by Andrew Ingham and Associates Ltd., photograph © Richard Waite
page 11, *Vitruvian Man*, c.1492, pen, ink, watercolor and metalpoint on paper, 34 x 25cm (13 x 10in), Gallerie dell'Accademia, Venice, Italy © Bettmann/Corbis
page 12, *The Last Supper*, c.1495-98, tempera on gesso, pitch and mastic, 460 x 880cm (181 x 346in), Convent of Santa Maria delle Grazie, Milan, Italy © The Art Gallery Collection/Alamy
page 12, red chalk sketches of horses, © Dennis Hallinan/Alamy
page 13, *Mona Lisa*, c.1503-6, oil on poplar panel, 77 x 53cm (30 x 21in), Louvre, Paris, France © The Art Archive/Musée du Louvre Paris/Collection Dagli Orti

ALBRECHT DÜRER
page 14, *Self Portrait with Gloves*, 1498, oil on wood panel, 52 x 41cm (21 x 16in), Prado, Madrid, Spain © Corbis
page 14, *View of Nuremburg*, 1496-97, watercolor on paper, 163 x 344cm (63½ x 134in), Kunsthalle, Bremen, Germany © Bridgeman Art Library
page 15, *Rhinoceros*, 1515, woodcut print, 25 x 30cm (10 x 12in), British Museum, London, UK © INTERFOTO/Alamy
page 15, *A Young Hare*, 1502, watercolor and gouache on paper, 25 x 23cm (10 x 9in), Graphische Sammlung Albertina, Vienna, Austria © The Gallery Collection/Corbis

MICHELANGELO
page 16, *Portrait of Michelangelo* by Jacopino del Conte, Casa Buonarroti, Florence, Italy © 2011 Photo Scala, Florence
page 16, *David*, c.1501-4, marble, height 517cm (203½in), Galleria dell'Accademia, Florence, Italy © Summerfield Press/Corbis

page 16, sketch for *David*, ink on paper, 37 x 19.5 cm (15 x 8in), Louvre, Paris, France © The Art Gallery Collection/Alamy
page 17, *The Holy Family*, c.1506, tempera on wood panel, diameter 120cm (47in), Uffizi Gallery, Florence, Italy © akg-images/Rabatti - Domingie
page 18, Sistine Chapel ceiling, Vatican City, c.1508-12, frescoes © LOOK Die Bildagentur der Fotografen GmbH/Alamy

RAPHAEL
page 19, *Self Portrait*, c.1506, tempera on wood panel, 47.5 x 33cm (19 x 13in), Uffizi Gallery, Florence, Italy © akg-images/Cameraphoto
page 19, photo of Raphael's house in Urbino © Bridgeman Art Library
page 19, black chalk sketch of a cherub, Palais des Beaux-Arts, Lille, France © RMN/Jacques Quecq d'Henripret
page 20, *St. George and the Dragon*, c.1504, oil on wood panel, 31 x 27cm (12 x 11in), Louvre, Paris, France © 2011 Photo Scala, Florence
page 21, *The Alba Madonna*, c.1510, oil on wood panel transferred to canvas, diameter 94.5cm (37in), National Gallery of Art, Washington DC, USA © Francis G. Mayer/Corbis

TITIAN
page 22, *Self Portrait*, c.1560, oil on canvas, 86 x 65cm (34 x 26in), Prado, Madrid, Spain © The Art Gallery Collection/Alamy
page 22, *Flora*, c.1520, oil on canvas, 80 x 63.5cm (31 x 25in), Uffizi Gallery, Florence, Italy © Bridgeman Art Library
page 23, *Bacchus and Ariadne*, c.1523, oil on canvas, 176.5 x 191cm (69½ x 75in), National Gallery, London, UK © The Print Collector/Alamy

HANS HOLBEIN
page 24, *Self Portrait*, 1542, pastel on paper, 32 x 26cm (12½ x 10in), Uffizi Gallery, Florence, Italy © 2011 Photo Scala, Florence – courtesy of the Ministero Beni e Att. Culturali
page 24, sketch of Ambrosius and Hans Holbein, by Hans Holbein the Elder, brown ink over silverpoint on paper, National Museums, Berlin © 2011 Photo Scala, Florence/BPK, Bildagentur fuer Kunst, Kultur und Geschichte, Berlin

page 25, design for a gold cup, ink and gold on paper, Ashmolean Museum, University of Oxford, UK © Bridgeman Art Library

page 25, *The Ambassadors*, 1533, oil on oak, 207 x 209.5cm (81 x 82in), The National Gallery, London, UK © 2011 The National Gallery, London/Scala, Florence

BRUEGEL

page 26, self portrait sketch, *The Painter and the Art Lover*, c.1565, ink on paper, 25.5 x 21.5cm (10 x 8½in), Graphische Sammlung Albertina, Vienna, Austria © akg-images

page 26, *Big Fish Eat Little Fish*, 1556, pen and ink on paper, 23 x 30cm (9 x 12in), Graphische Sammlung Albertina, Vienna, Austria © akg-images

page 27, photo of Brussels © Bernal Revert/Alamy

page 27, *Winter Landscape with Skaters and a Bird Trap*, 1565, oil on panel, 38 x 56cm (15 x 22in), private collection © Giraudon/Bridgeman Art Library

EL GRECO

page 28, *Portrait of An Old Man*, c.1590 –1600, oil on canvas, 53 x 47cm (20½ x 18in) Metropolitan Museum of Art, New York, USA © 2011 Metropolitan Museum of Art/Art Resource/Scala, Florence

page 28, photo of a reconstruction of El Greco's studio in the El Greco House and Museum, Toledo, Spain © Sheldan Collins/Corbis

page 29, photo of Toledo © Manuel Cohen/ Getty Images

page 29, *The Burial of Count Orgaz*, 1586, 460 x 360cm (180 x 140in), oil on canvas, Church of Santo Tomé, Toledo, Spain © 2011 Photo Scala, Florence

CARAVAGGIO

page 30, *Portrait of Caravaggio* by Ottavia Leoni, c.1621, red and black pencil, Marucelliana Library, Florence, Italy © 2011 Photo Scala, Florence

page 30, *The Basket of Fruit*, c.1596, 31 x 47cm (12 x 18in), oil on canvas, Ambrosian Library, Milan, Italy © Bridgeman Art Library

page 31, *Supper at Emmaus*, 1601, oil and tempera on canvas, 141 x 196cm (56 x 76½in), National Gallery, London, UK © Bridgeman Art Library, London/ SuperStock

PETER PAUL RUBENS

page 32, *Self Portrait*, c.1618, oil on panel, 78 x 61cm (30½ x 24in), Uffizi Gallery, Florence, Italy © Summerfield Press/Corbis

page 33, *Self Portrait with Isabella Brant*, 1609, oil on canvas, 178 x 136.5cm (69½ x 53in), Alte Pinakothek Gallery, Munich, Germany © 2011 Photo Scala, Florence/ BPK, Bildagentur fuer Kunst, Kultur und Geschichte, Berlin

page 33, *Sketch of Nicolas* © Graphische Sammlung Albertina, Vienna, Austria/ Bridgeman Art Library

page 34, *The Coronation of Marie de Medici at Saint-Denis*, 1622-25, oil on canvas, 394 x 727cm (153½ x 283½in), Louvre, Paris, France © 2011 Photo Scala, Florence

REMBRANDT

page 35, *Self Portrait*, 1629, 15.5 x 13cm (6 x 5in) oil on panel, Alte Pinakothek, Munich, Germany © The Art Gallery Collection/Alamy

page 35, *Dam Square, Amsterdam, 1659*, by Jacob van der Ulft © The Art Archive/ Musée Condé Chantilly/Gianni Dagli Orti

page 36, red chalk sketch of Saskia with her first child © Samuel Courtauld Trust, The Courtauld Gallery, London, UK/ Bridgeman Art Library

page 36, *The Night Watch*, 1642, oil on canvas, 363 x 437cm (141½ x 170½in), Rijksmuseum, Amsterdam, The Netherlands © Corbis

page 37, *Self Portrait at the Age of 63*, 1669, oil on canvas, 86 x 70.5cm (33½ x 28in), National Gallery, London, UK © The Art Gallery Collection/Alamy

DIEGO VELÁZQUEZ

page 38, *The Maids of Honor*, (and detail showing self portrait), c.1656, oil on canvas, 316 x 276cm (123 x 107½in), Prado, Madrid, Spain © 2011 Photo Scala, Florence

page 39, *Portrait of Pope Innocent X*, oil on canvas 140 x 120cm (54½ x 47in), Galleria Doria Pamphilj, Rome, Italy © Alinari/Bridgeman Art Library

JAN VERMEER

page 40, detail showing self portrait from *The Procuress*, 1656, oil on canvas, 143 x 130cm (56 x 51in), Old Masters Picture Gallery, Dresden, Germany © World History Archive/Alamy

page 40, *View of Delft*, c.1660-61, oil on canvas, 98 x 117.5cm (39 x 46½in), Mauritshuis, The Hague, The Netherlands © The Gallery Collection/Corbis

page 41, *The Artist's Studio*, c.1665-66, oil on canvas, 120 x 100cm (47 x 39in), Kunsthistorisches Museum, Vienna, Austria © Francis G. Mayer/Corbis

GOYA

page 42, *Self Portrait with Glasses*, c.1788-98, oil on canvas, 61 x 47cm (24 x 18in) Goya Museum, Castres, France © Bridgeman Art Library

page 42, *The Sleep of Reason Produces Monsters*, 1797-98, etching, 22 x 15cm (8½ x 6in), British Museum, London, UK © Burstein Collection/Corbis

page 43, *Third of May 1808*, 1814, oil on canvas, 268 x 347 (105½ x 137in) Prado, Madrid, Spain © Masterpics/Alamy

J.M.W. TURNER

page 44, *Portrait of Turner*, Victoria and Albert Museum, London, UK © V&A Images

page 44, pages from Turner's sketchbook © Yale Center for British Art, London, Paul Mellon Collection, USA/Bridgeman Art Library

page 45, *The Fighting Temeraire*, 1839, oil on canvas, 91 x 122cm (35½ x 47½ in), The National Gallery, London, UK © Bridgeman Art Library, London/SuperStock

EUGÈNE DELACROIX

page 46, Caricature of Delacroix by Eugène Giraud, watercolor, pencil and gouache on paper, Musée de la Ville de Paris, Musée Carnavalet, Paris, France © Archives Charmet/Bridgeman Art Library

page 46, *Liberty Leading the People*, 1830, oil on canvas, 260 x 325cm (103 x 128in), Louvre, Paris, France © The Gallery Collection/Corbis

page 47, pages from Delacroix's sketchbook, 1832, watercolor on paper, Musée Condé, Chantilly, France © Giraudon/Bridgeman Art Library

JOHN EVERETT MILLAIS

page 48, *Self Portrait*, 1847, oil on board, 27 x 22cm (11 x 8½in), Walker Art Gallery, Liverpool, UK © Walker Art Gallery, National Museums Liverpool/Bridgeman Art Library

page 49, *Ophelia*, 1852, oil on canvas, 70 x 110cm (27 x 39in), Tate Britain, London, UK © The Art Archive/Tate Gallery London/ Eileen Tweedy

page 49, Millais in his drawing room, c.1890 © Hulton Archive/Getty Images

EDOUARD MANET

page 50, *Portrait of Manet* by Henri de Fantin-Latour, 1867, 117 x 90cm (46 x 35in) Art Institute of Chicago, USA © 2011 White Images/Scala, Florence

page 50, illustration for 'The Raven' by Edgar Allen Poe, 1875, On loan to the Hamburg Kunsthalle, Hamburg, Germany © Bridgeman Art Library

page 51, *A Bar at the Folies Bergères*, 1882, oil on canvas, 96 x 130cm (37½ x 51in), Courtauld Institute Galleries, London © 2011 White Images/Scala, Florence

EDGAR DEGAS

page 52, *Self Portrait in a Brown Vest*, 1856, oil on paper, 24 x 19cm (9½ x 7½in) The Pierpont Morgan Library, New York, USA © 2011 Photo Pierpont Morgan Library/Art Resource/Scala, Florence

page 52, crayon drawing of a jockey on horseback, The Barnes Foundation, Merion, Pennsylvania, USA © Bridgeman Art Library

page 53, *Dancers in the Classroom*, c.1880, oil on canvas, 39 x 88cm (15½ x 35in), Sterling and Francine Clark Art Institute, Williamstown, USA © Bridgeman Art Library

page 53, *Little Dancer Aged 14*, 1880-81, bronze with gauze tutu and silk ribbon on wooden base, height 99cm (39in), Sterling and Francine Clark Art Institute, Williamstown, USA © Bridgeman Art Library

CLAUDE MONET

page 54, *Self Portrait with a Beret*, 1886, oil on canvas, 56 x 46cm (22 x 18in), Private Collection. Photo: © Lefevre Fine Art Ltd., London/Bridgeman Art Library

page 54, Caricature of Félix, 1855-60, pencil on paper, Musée Marmottan, Paris, France © Giraudon/Bridgeman Art Library

page 55, photo of Monet's palette, Musée Marmottan, Paris, France © Giraudon/ Bridgeman Art Library

page 55, *Woman with a Parasol – Madame Monet and Her Son*, 1875, oil on canvas, 100 x 81cm (39 x 32in), National Gallery of Art, Washington DC, USA © AISA/Bridgeman Art Library

page 56, photo of Monet in his garden, © Mary Evans Picture Library

page 56, photo of Monet's glasses, Musée Marmottan, Paris, France © Giraudon/ Bridgeman Art Library

page 57, *Water Lilies at Giverny*, 1917, oil on canvas, 100 x 200cm (39 x 78in), Musée des Beaux-Arts, Nantes, France © Giraudon/ Bridgeman Art Library

page 57, photo of Monet in his studio by Henri Manuel © Roger-Viollet, Paris/ Bridgeman Art Library

PIERRE-AUGUSTE RENOIR

page 58, photo of Renoir, 1885 © Archives Charmet/Bridgeman Art Library

page 58, chalk sketches of a little child, 1875-80 © Fitzwilliam Museum, University of Cambridge, UK/Bridgeman Art Library

page 59, *Luncheon of the Boating Party*, Pierre-Auguste Renoir, 1880-81, oil on canvas, 130 x 176cm (51 x 69in), Phillips Collection, Washington DC, USA © The Gallery Collection/Corbis

page 59, photo of Renoir in his studio, 1914 © Edimédia/Corbis

PAUL CÉZANNE

page 60, photo of Cezanne, c.1903 © Bridgeman Art Library

page 60, *Still Life with Oranges and Apples*, 1899, oil on canvas, 74 x 93cm (29 x 37in), Musée d'Orsay, Paris, France © 2011 Photo Scala, Florence

page 61, photo of the mountain of St. Victoire © Gail Mooney/Corbis

page 61, *The Mountain of Sainte-Victoire*, 1900, oil on canvas, 78 x 99cm (31 x 39in), Hermitage, St. Petersburg, Russia © The Gallery Collection/Corbis

PAUL GAUGUIN

page 62, photo of Gauguin playing the harmonium © Mucha Trust/Bridgeman Art Library

page 62, *Breton Girls Dancing, Pont-Aven*, 1888, oil on canvas, 73 x 93cm (29 x 36½in), National Gallery of Art, Washington DC, USA © Corbis

page 63, pages from Gauguin's sketchbook, © RMN (Musée d'Orsay)/Hervé Lewandowski

page 63, photo of Gauguin's home in Tahiti, © Morton Beebe/Corbis

page 64, *Where Do We Come From? What Are We? Where Are We Going?*, 1897, oil on canvas, 139 x 375cm (54 x 146in) Museum of Fine Arts, Boston, Massachusetts, USA © Tompkins Collection/Bridgeman Art Library

page 64, photo of Gauguin's grave © Douglas Peebles Photography/Alamy

VINCENT VAN GOGH

page 65, *Self Portrait as an Artist*, 1888, oil on canvas, 65.5 x 50.5cm (25½ x 18in), Van Gogh Museum, Amsterdam, The Netherlands © SuperStock/SuperStock

page 65, pages from a letter from from Vincent to his brother Theo van Gogh, 1881, ink and pencil © Van Gogh Museum Amsterdam (Vincent van Gogh Foundation)

page 66, pen and ink sketch of van Gogh's house in Arles, photo: © Christie's Images/ Bridgeman Art Library

page 66, *The Bedroom at Arles*, 1889, oil on canvas 57.5 x 74cm (22½ x 29in), Musée d'Orsay, Paris, France © The Art Archive/Musée d'Orsay Paris/Collection Dagli Orti

page 67, *Wheatfield with Crows*, 1890, oil on canvas, 50.5 x 103cm (20 x 40in), Van Gogh Museum, Amsterdam, The Netherlands © Francis G. Mayer/Corbis

page 67, photo of van Gogh's paint tubes © RMN (Musée d'Orsay)/Droits réservés

GUSTAV KLIMT

page 68, photo of Klimt with his cat, c.1912, © 2011 Austrian Archives/Scala Florence

page 68, *Secession poster* © Austrian Archives/Corbis

page 69, photo of Klimt and Emilie Flöge © Imagno/Getty Images

page 69, *The Kiss*, 1907-1908, oil on canvas, 180 x 180cm (70 x 70in) Belvedere Gallery, Vienna © 2011 photo Austrian Archives/ Scala Florence

HENRI MATISSE

page 70, photo of Matisse in his studio, 1913 © Getty Images

page 70, photo of Collioure, France © photo Jean-Pierre Lescourret/Corbis

page 70, *The Roofs of Collioure*, 1905, oil on canvas, 60 x 73cm (23½ x 28½), Hermitage Museum, St. Petersburg, Russia. Photo: Archives Henri Matisse. © Succession H. Matisse/DACS 2011

page 71, *Harmony in Red*, 1908, oil on canvas, 180 x 220cm (71 x 87in), Hermitage Museum, St. Petersburg, Russia. Photo: Archives Henri Matisse. © Succession H.

Matisse/DACS 2011

page 71, photo of Matisse painting a mural
Photo: © The Barnes Foundation, Merion, Pennsylvania, USA/Bridgeman Art Library

page 72, *Woman with a Purple Coat*, 1937, oil on canvas, 81 x 65cm (31½ x 25in) Museum of Fine Arts, Houston, Texas, USA, Gift of Audrey Jones Beck
Photo: © Bridgeman Art Library.
© Succession H. Matisse/DACS 2011

page 73, *Icarus*, from the illustrated book, *Jazz*, 1943. Photo: Archives Henri Matisse.
© Succession H. Matisse/DACS 2011

page 73, photo of Matisse working in bed, 1949 © Condé Nast Archive/Corbis

WASSILY KANDINSKY

page 74, photo of Kandinsky painting, 1936 © Roger-Viollet, Paris/Bridgeman Art Library © ADAGP, Paris/DACS, London 2011

page 74, photo of Kandinsky's palette, private collection © Giraudon/Bridgeman Art Library

page 75, *Composition No. 6*, 1913, oil on canvas, 195 x 300cm (76 x 117in), Hermitage Museum, St. Petersburg, Russia © 2011 Photo Scala, Florence, © ADAGP, Paris/DACS, London 2011

page 75, photo of the mural studio storeroom, from the workshops of the Bauhaus, Weimar, 1923 © The Stapleton Collection/Bridgeman Art Library

PABLO PICASSO

page 76, signed photo of Picasso, 1904, Musée de Montmartre, Paris, France © Archives Charmet/Bridgeman Art Library

page 76, photo of Montmartre Boulevard, c.1900 © Bettmann/Corbis

page 77, *Acrobat and Young Harlequin*, 1905, oil on canvas, 190 x 108cm (74 x 42in), The Barnes Foundation, Merion, Pennsylvania, USA © Bridgeman Art Library

page 77, *Mother and child* (Olga & Paulo), 1922, pen and ink, Haags Gemeentemuseum, The Hague, The Netherlands © Bridgeman Art Library

page 78, photo by Dora Maar of Picasso working on *Guernica* © DACS/Archives Charmet/Bridgeman Art Library, © ADAGP, Paris and DACS, London 2011

page 78, *Guernica*, 1937, oil on canvas, 350 x 782cm (136½ x 305in) Museo Nacional Centro de Arte Reina Sofia,

Madrid, Spain © 2011 photo Art Resource/Scala, Florence/John Bigelow Taylor

page 79, plate bearing a profile portrait of Jacqueline Picasso, 1962, diameter 43.5cm (17in) © Photo: Bonhams, London, UK/Bridgeman Art Library

page 79, photo of Picasso in his studio with Brigitte Bardot © Photo by Jerome Brierre/RDA/Getty Images

All pictures (except photo of Montmartre Boulevard) © Succession Picasso/DACS, London 2011

EDWARD HOPPER

page 80, photo of Hopper in his studio © Time & Life Pictures/Getty Images

page 80, *Automat*, 1927, oil on canvas 71.5 x 91.5cm (28 x 36in), Des Moines Art Center, Des Moines, USA © Francis G. Mayer/Corbis

page 81, *The House by the Railroad*, 1925, oil on canvas, 61 x 74cm (24 x 29in), The Museum of Modern Art, New York, USA © 2011 Digital image, The Museum of Modern Art, New York/Scala, Florence

page 81, Addams Family Cartoon – Boiling Oil, Tee & Charles Addams Foundation, © Charles Addams. With permission Tee and Charles Addams Foundation

RENÉ MAGRITTE

page 82, photo of Magritte with an apple © 2011 BI, ADAGP, Paris/Scala, Florence

page 82, photo of Magritte and friends © 2011 BI, ADAGP, Paris/Scala, Florence

page 82, *This is not a Pipe*, 1929, oil on canvas, 64.5 x 94cm (25 x 37in), Los Angeles County Museum of Art, USA © 2011 Digital Image Museum Associates/LACMA/Art Resource NY/Scala, Florence

page 83 *The Mysterious Barricades*, 1961, 527 x 870cm (205 x 339in), Palace of Congress, Brussels, Belgium © 2011 BI, ADAGP, Paris/Scala, Florence
All pictures © ADAGP, Paris/DACS, London 2011

SALVADOR DALÍ

page 84, photo of Dalí with a magnified eye © Hulton-Deutsch Collection/Corbis

page 84, photo of Dalí painting © Bettmann/Corbis

page 85, *The Persistence of Memory*, 1931, oil on canvas, 24 x 33cm (9½ x 13in), Museum of Modern Art, New York, USA © 2011 Digital image, The Museum of

Modern Art, New York/Scala, Florence
All pictures © Salvador Dali, Fundació Gala-Salvador Dalí, DACS, 2011

JACKSON POLLOCK

page 86, photo of Pollock painting © Everett Collection/Rex Features

pages 86-87, *Blue Poles*, 1952, oil, enamel, aluminium paint & glass on canvas, 212 x 489cm (83 x 191in), National Gallery of Australia, Canberra. Photo: © DACS/Purchased 1973/Bridgeman Art Library. Artwork: © The Pollock-Krasner Foundation ARS, NY and DACS, London 2011

page 87, photo of the floor of Pollock's studio © Susan Wood/Getty Images

ANDY WARHOL

page 88, photo of Warhol in his studio, © Bob Adelman/Corbis

page 88, *Sam*, 1954, 23 x 15cm (9 x 6in) © The Andy Warhol Foundation/Corbis

page 88 photo of Warhol and friends in the Factory © Steve Schapiro/Corbis

page 89, *One Hundred Campbell's Soup Cans*, screenprinted paint on canvas, 183 x 132cm (72 x 52in), Albright-Knox Art Gallery, Buffalo, USA © The Andy Warhol Foundation/Corbis
All pictures © The Andy Warhol Foundation for the Visual Arts/Artists Rights Society (ARS), New York/DACS, London 2011

Index

abstract art, 74, 81, 90
Addams Family, 81
advertising, 85, 88
Amsterdam, 35
Antwerp, 26, 32
architecture, 7, 16, 17, 18, 20, 75
Arena Chapel, Padua, 7
Arles, 66
Augsburg, 24

Bauhaus, 75
Braque, Georges, 77
Bruegel, Pieter, 26-27
Bruges, 8
Brussels, 27, 82, 83

camera obscura, 41
Caravaggio, 30-31
caricatures, 46, 54
ceramics, 76, 79
Cézanne, Paul, 29, 60-61
Chapel of the Rosary, Vence, 73
Charles I, King of England, 33
cherubs, 19
chiaroscuro, 31
collages, 76
Collioure, 70
Crete, 28
Cubism, 77

Dalí, Salvador, 84-85
Degas, Edgar, 51, 52-53
Delacroix, Eugène, 46-47
Delft, 40, 41
Dürer, Albrecht, 14-15

El Greco, 28-29
Erasmus, Desiderius, 24
exhibitions, 46, 50, 53, 54, 56, 58,
   60, 61, 68, 71, 81, 82, 89

fauve, 71
Figueres, 85

filmmaking, 80, 84, 89
First World War, 75
Florence, 6, 7, 11, 16, 17, 19, 20

Gauguin, Paul, 62-64, 65, 66
Giotto, 6-7,
Giverny, 56, 57
Gonzaga, Vincenzo I,
   Duke of Mantua, 32
Goya, 42-43

Henry VIII, King of England,
   24, 25
Holbein, Hans, 24-25
Hopper, Edward, 80-81

illustration, 50, 80, 88, 90
impasto, 36
Impressionists, 47, 51, 52-59
Innocent X, Pope, 39
inventions, 10, 11, 18

Kandinsky, Wassily, 74-75
Klimt, Gustav, 68-69

landscapes, 8, 9, 14 26, 27, 40, 44,
   45, 47, 61, 67, 69, 70
Le Havre, 54
Leiden, 35
Leonardo da Vinci, 10-13,
   19, 20
London, 24, 33, 44
Lyons, 26

Madrid, 42, 84
Magritte, René, 82-83
Malta, 31
Manet, Edouard, 29, 50-51
Mantua, 32
Marquesas Islands, the, 64
Mathematics, 11,
Matisse, Henri, 70-73
Medici, Marie de, 34
Michelangelo, 11, 16-18, 19, 20, 28
Milan, 11, 12

Millais, John Everett, 48-49
Monet, Claude, 51, 53, 54-57, 58
Morocco, 47
mythology as subject, 22, 23,
   26, 34, 36

Naples, 26, 31,
Netherlands, 8, 26, 40
New York, 56, 80, 81, 86, 87
Nice, 72, 73
nudes, 22, 50, 51, 68
Nuremberg, 14

paints,
   oil, 8, 44, 84
   watercolor, 14, 44
Paris, 50, 52, 54, 58, 60, 62, 64,
   65, 66, 70, 71, 76, 82, 83, 84
Philip III, King of Spain, 32
Philip II, King of Spain, 29
Philip IV, King of Spain, 38, 39
Picasso, Pablo, 29, 61, 76-79
Pollock, Jackson, 86-87
Pont-Aven, 62, 63
portraits, 6, 8, 9, 13, 16, 22, 23,
   24, 25, 35, 36, 38, 39, 42, 44,
   50, 58, 79
pottery, see ceramics
Pre-Raphaelite Brotherhood,
   48, 49
prints, 14, 15, 24, 42, 43, 73,
   79, 89
putti, 19

Raphael, 11, 19-21, 48
religious subjects, 6, 7, 8, 9, 12,
   17, 18, 19, 20, 21, 28, 30, 31
Rembrandt, 35-37
Renoir, Pierre-August, 51, 54,
   58-59
Riley, Bridget, 90-91
Rome, 6, 13, 17, 18, 20, 26, 28,
   30, 31,
Royal Academy, London, 44,
   48, 49

Rubens, Peter Paul, 32-34, 39
Ruskin, John, 48

Salon (Paris), 50, 51
screenprinting, 89
sculptures, 12, 16, 53, 71, 76,
   84, 89
Secession, 68
Second World War, 72, 75, 79, 90
self portraits, 8, 9, 10, 14, 19, 22,
   24, 26, 28, 32, 33, 35, 37, 38,
   40, 42, 48, 52, 65
Seville, 38
Sicily, 31
Sistine Chapel, 17, 18, 21
sketches, 10, 11, 12, 14, 16, 36,
   44, 47, 52, 54, 58, 63, 65, 66
Spanish Civil War, 78
still lifes, 30, 60
Surrealists, 82-85

Tahiti, 63, 64
tapestries, 20, 21, 42
Titian, 22-23, 32
Toledo, 28
Turner, J.M.W., 44-45

van Eyck, Jan, 8-9
van Gogh, Theo, 65, 67
van Gogh, Vincent, 65-67
Velázquez, Diego, 38-39
Venice, 22, 23, 32
Vermeer, Jan, 40-41
Victoria, Queen of Britain, 49
Vienna, 68, 69

wall paintings, 6, 7, 12, 13, 21, 22,
   68, 71, 73
war, as subject, 43, 46, 78
Warhol, Andy, 88-89

Zaragoza, 42

Edited by Jane Chisholm, Cover design by Mary Cartwright, Picture research by Ruth King
American editor: Carrie Armstrong

Every effort has been made to trace the copyright holders of the material in this book. If any rights have been omitted,
the publishers offer their sincere apologies and will rectify this in any subsequent editions following notification. The publishers are grateful
to the organizations and individuals named above for their contributions and permission to reproduce material.

Usborne Pulishing Ltd. has paid DACS' visual creators for the use of their artistic works.